Acknowledgements

With thanks to our clients and colleagues with whom we gained the valuable experience to write this book.

YOU'RE HIRED! PSYCHOMETRIC TESTS

PROVEN TACTICS TO HELP YOU PASS

CERI RODERICK AND JAMES MEACHIN

You're Hired! Psychometric Tests: proven tactics to help you pass

This edition first published in 2010 by Trotman Publishing, a division of Crimson Publishing Ltd., Westminster House, Kew Road, Richmond, Surrey TW9 2ND

Authors Ceri Roderick and James Meachin

British Library Cataloguing in Publication Data
A catalogue record for this book is available from the British Library

ISBN 978 1 8445 5 230 6

Printed and bound in Great Britain by TJ International Ltd, Padstow, Cornwall

CONTENTS

LIST OF ACTIVITIES

ABOUT THE AUTHORS

Ceri Roderick is a partner and Head of Assessment at Pearn Kandola, with over 25 years' experience in using psychometric tests. After a period with Deloittes, he joined Pearn Kandola in 2000, and works with blue chip companies and government departments, nationally and internationally, on all aspects of assessment.

James Meachin is Principal Psychologist at the business psychology consulting firm Pearn Kandola, where he specialises in the design and delivery of assessment processes. He is a chartered occupational psychologist and holds a master's degree from Cardiff University.

INTRODUCTION

On the basis that knowledge reduces fear and fear reduces performance, our aim is to give you expert guidance on how to approach
psychometric tests. Between us, we have over 30 years' experience in
designing, interpreting and using psychometric tests to help make employment
decisions for our client organisations. Over this time, we have used psychometric tests to recruit candidates for a diverse range of roles – from board directors
to shopfloor workers and everything in between. In doing so, we have worked
with many of the world's largest organisations as well as many smaller, regional
businesses.

In this book we have distilled our knowledge and experience to help you to
maximise your ability to take, and pass, psychometric tests. The principles we
have outlined will be useful for any test taker, and the content of this book is
intended to be applicable to as wide a range of job applicants as possible.

As we take you through the world of psychometric tests we present examples
from a variety of test types, pitched at a wide range of difficulty levels. Whether
you are a first-time applicant looking to enter a graduate training scheme, or a
highly experienced executive exploring new avenues, we will guide you through
the process of test taking.

How to get the best from this book

Do you know which types of psychometric test you will be asked to take the
next time you apply for a job? There are specific chapters dealing with each

of the major test types – numerical reasoning (Chapter 2), verbal reasoning (Chapter 3), abstract reasoning (Chapter 4) and preference tests (Chapter 6). In addition, Chapter 5 covers the knowledge and skill tests that you might encounter. If you wish, dive straight in and read the chapter about the kind of test(s) that you will be taking. As well as very practical advice you will find example questions pitched at different levels of difficulty. Simply by getting more familiar with the test formats, your confidence will quickly increase and your performance will improve.

What about the other chapters? In our experience psychometric tests are often the least understood, and therefore the least comfortable part of the job application process. However, the fundamentals are surprisingly simple and we have outlined these in Chapter 1, 'What is a psychometric test?'. As with any discipline, once the basics have been demystified you will feel a great deal more confident in your own ability. Likewise, Chapter 7, 'Performing at your best', covers everything you will need to know about test preparation and test taking. This is crucial because, as our experience shows, although it takes a great deal of time to improve your true level of ability, there are many practical steps you can quickly take to ensure that you perform to the very best of your ability. As part of your becoming an informed and savvy test taker, we also tackle the common myths and misconceptions that surround psychometric tests and which are invariably unhelpful and often inaccurate. In this book, we put these issues to rest by giving you a comprehensive low-down on how psychometric tests work and how they are used by employers to make hiring decisions.

Whichever psychometric tests you take in the future, the insight and advice in this book will ensure that you are as well prepared as you can be. We would wish you luck, but instead we offer the reminder that the harder you prepare, the luckier you will be.

1 WHAT IS A PSYCHOMETRIC TEST?

This chapter will help you to get to grips with the basics of psychometric testing, so that you become a more informed and confident test taker. As a candidate you will understand:

■ The different types of psychometric test

■ How psychometric tests work

■ How employers use psychometric tests to make decisions

What is psychometric testing?

Psychometric tests provide a measure that employers can use to understand certain aspects of your mind. At first that might sound rather spooky. However, as you will see, there is no 'black magic' involved and, best of all, no invasive procedures are used!

In fact, far from the obscure old-world psychological tests involving ink blots, modern psychometric tests are transparent, objective measures, where each candidate has the same experience and opportunity to perform. Instead of vague interpretations, psychometric tests produce clear outcomes which give recruiters valuable information about you and your abilities.

How do psychometric tests 'measure' people?

If you want to know how tall someone is you would use a metric such as centimetres. Psychometric tests also use a metric to tell us 'how much' of a particular quality someone has. If we want to know who is taller out of the two, John or Chloe, we can measure both and compare the difference. In the same way, psychometric tests allow employers to make direct comparisons between candidates.

Psychometric tests allow employers to make direct comparisons between candidates

Psychometric tests work by comparing your responses with other people's answers – known as a comparison group. Each comparison group is usually made up of hundreds or thousands of people who are in a particular country and have reached a certain educational or occupational level. The information about comparison groups is provided to hiring organisations by the publisher.

How does this work in practice? See the case studies over the page.

Case study – Comparison groups
German graduates

Michael is based in Germany and is applying for his first job with a graduate recruiter. The company compares Michael's scores on a psychometric test he took with other German graduates. Michael's score is expressed as a 'percentile'. If Michael's score is on the 50th percentile, the employer knows that he is exactly average in comparison with his German peers, i.e. 50% score lower than him and 50% score higher. In fact, Michael is on the 65th percentile, so he has performed better than 64% of his fellow German graduates.

UK senior managers and professionals

Sophie is based in the UK and is applying for a role as the head of research and development at a pharmaceutical company. Sophie's test scores are compared with those of a group of senior managers and professionals within the UK. Notice that this comparison group is at a similar level of seniority to Sophie, although it is not industry specific. This is the most common approach in psychometric testing, although some employers, in highly specialised sectors such as investment banking, will use very specific comparison groups based on their own sector or organisation.

In essence, remember that psychometric tests work by comparing your answers with the answers given by other, similar people.

What do psychometric tests measure?

In principle, a psychometric test could be designed to measure almost any aspect of your mind. But that's a lot of ground to cover, so let's keep this simple. Employers use psychometric tests to measure two broad categories of qualities – abilities and preferences. The main differences between ability tests and preference tests are shown in Table 1.1

Table 1.1

Ability tests	Preference tests
Include reasoning with numbers, words or diagrams	Include personality, values and integrity questionnaires
There are absolute right and wrong answers	There is no one 'correct' answer to a question
Usually have a time limit	Are generally untimed

Ability tests

Ability tests are tests of numerical reasoning (see Chapter 2), verbal reasoning (Chapter 3), abstract reasoning (Chapter 4) and specific types of skills and knowledge (Chapter 5). When used for recruitment, ability tests can serve two purposes. The first is to help employers understand how capable you are at demonstrating a specific skill that is relevant to the job you are applying for. See the case study below.

Case study – Testing specific abilities

Oliver is applying for a graduate position at a major accountancy firm. The firm uses a test of numerical reasoning ability. As the name implies, the questions in this test measure Oliver's ability to use and reason with numbers, for example, by performing calculations, interpreting sets of numbers, and checking for differences. Because work as a trainee ac-countant involves these types of task, Oliver's results tell the employer something useful about his ability to do well in the job. If Oliver's score is on the 15th percentile, then the employer would know that many more graduates will be better than him at working with numerical data.

Employers can also use ability tests to measure your overall level of intelligence. This is useful because more intelligent people tend to be quicker learners and are generally better at solving complex problems. See the case study below for more details.

Case study – Testing general intelligence

Samantha is applying for a position at a management consulting firm, which uses ability tests for checking out applicants' general intelligence. The firm's consultants need to get to grips with new clients very quickly and understand how they operate. They have to solve problems and present solutions to their clients, who are often working in sectors and markets that the consultants may not be familiar with. As part of her application, Samantha is asked to complete verbal and numerical reasoning tests. While both of these abilities are relevant to the role of a management consultant, the firm is more interested in her overall intelligence, which it estimates by combining the scores on both tests. Her combined score is on the 80th percentile, so the firm can be very confident about employing her intellectual capacity.

How can psychometric tests measure specific abilities like numerical reasoning and verbal reasoning as well as something called general intelligence? It all comes down to the relationship – the correlation – between different abilities. Think back to school. Were the people who were good at one subject also good at others? Generally, the answer is 'yes'. This is because of general intelligence. Different mental abilities correlate well, and this is shown by the overlapping circles in the diagram opposite. Each circle covers some unique ground – this is information only that test provides. The accountancy firm that Oliver applied to was only concerned with numerical ability. For this reason they only needed a numerical reasoning test. In contrast the management consulting firm was interested in measuring general intelligence and so they used two tests. This meant that they had a more accurate assessment of candidates' overall intelligence.

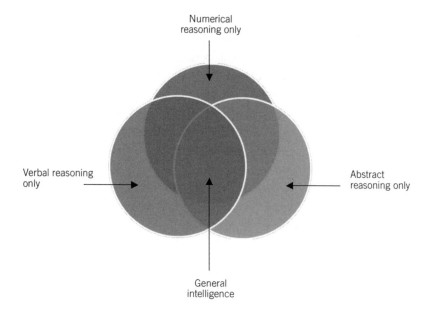

Numerical
reasoning only

Verbal reasoning
only

Abstract
reasoning only

General
intelligence

Whatever reason employers have for using psychometric ability tests, you can see from the case studies that your test scores will directly affect hiring decisions. Later on in this chapter, we will describe how employers use psychometric test scores to reach hiring decisions.

Preference tests

Now let's look at the psychometric tests that measure preferences. The most common type of preference test is a personality questionnaire. The idea behind these tests is that we are all reasonably consistent in our behaviour, and this is because our behaviours are shaped, in part, by our personality. Think about your own personality traits:

- Do you tend to arrive early or turn up late?
- Will you stay calm in a crisis or wear your heart on your sleeve?
- Are you naturally talkative or reserved in a crowd?

People who know you well will know what to expect from you – and could probably answer these questions on your behalf! Of course we all do different things on different occasions, but our behaviour is far from random. Our personality drives the preferences that shape our behaviour in one direction, and move us away from another direction. Employers are interested in measuring your personality because it provides them with information about your personal style – the sorts of tasks and activities that you naturally enjoy and those situations that you may wish to avoid.

So what do personality questionnaires actually measure? Usually the questions you answer will correspond to five broad domains. These are shown in Table 1.2 below, along with example questions.

Table 1.2

Personality domain	Example questions	Answer	
		Yes	No
Openness to experience	I prefer to have variety in my day		
	I enjoy hearing new ideas		
	I have a vivid imagination		
Conscientiousness	I like working towards a plan		
	I always keep my promises		
	I pay attention to the details		
Extraversion	I want to be the centre of attention		
	I like having lots to do		
	I enjoy being around other people		
Agreeableness	I believe that other people are trustworthy		
	I try to avoid getting into disagreements		
	I feel sorry for people less fortunate than me		

Personality domain	Example questions	Answer	
		Yes	No
Emotional stability	I rarely worry about things		
	I find it easy to get over setbacks		
	It takes a lot to make me feel angry		

When you complete a personality questionnaire you might wonder – most people do – why the same sorts of questions come up so regularly. Contrary to popular belief, this is not a cunning method to catch people out if they give different answers. In fact, you might well respond differently to similar questions and that's how the questionnaire works.

In the case study overleaf, Charlotte completed a personality questionnaire as part of a promotions process by a book publisher in Paris.

Case study – Matching the right personality to the job

Charlotte has taken a personality test that her employer uses to assess employees' suitability for a particular job. The test consisted of 20 statements describing different aspects of socialising or working with others (e.g. 'I quickly get bored when I am alone') and Charlotte had to indicate whether she agreed or disagreed with them. Charlotte tended to agree with statements about wanting to spend time with others and she tended to disagree with statements about spending time alone.

So is she an introvert (someone who is comfortable in her own company) or an extravert (someone who prefers to be around others)? That depends how her responses match-up with the comparison group. Her employer used a comparison group of 2,000 managers and professionals based in France. Because Charlotte endorsed more extravert-related questions than 80% of the comparison group, we can say that she has a strong preference towards extraversion.

Charlotte's colleagues Tomas and Sebastian also completed the questionnaire. Tomas endorsed some statements relating to extraversion and some statements about introversion. This does not mean that Tomas is indecisive, or, indeed, schizophrenic. In fact, most people prefer a balance between the two extremes of highly sociable or hermit-like. Because Tomas' responses were similar to many people in the comparison group he was close to the average, which is 50%. This shows that Tomas has a balanced preference, suggesting that there are times when he enjoys being with other people and times when he is comfortable in his own company.

Finally, Sebastian endorsed fewer questions relating to extraversion than either Tomas or Charlotte. Based on the comparison group he is on the 20th percentile for extraversion. This shows that Sebastian has a strong preference towards introversion.

It's important to note that personality test results are interpreted differently from the ability tests, where higher scores are better. In the above case study example, we cannot say that Charlotte is somehow 'better' than Tomas or Sebastian. What we can say is that she is more extraverted than most other managers and professionals working in France. Tomas has a similar level of extraversion to most managers and professionals, whilst Sebastian is more introverted than many of his peers.

Why employers use psychometric tests

There are two main reasons why employers use these tests early on in the selction process:

- **Cost-effectiveness** – ability-based psychometric tests can be completed online by candidates and automatically scored, without human intervention. Because the early stages of a recruitment process involve screening the largest number of candidates, employers prefer to use highly efficient selection methods, such as psychometric tests, which incur relatively small financial costs and no time costs. The figure below is an illustration of a typical recruitment process, showing where psychometric tests usually occur within a selection process.
- **Better assessment of candidates' suitability** – ability-based psychometric tests are, when used appropriately, among the best methods for predicting how well a candidate will perform on the job. It makes sense to use the most accurate selection tests early on because this is when the most candidates are screened out. By taking this approach employers reduce the number of unsuitable candidates who will attend the latter stages of a recruitment process, as well as avoiding mistakenly screening out suitable candidates.

A typical recruitment process

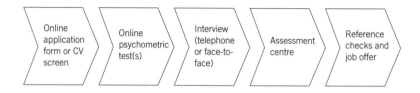

Online application form or CV screen → Online psychometric test(s) → Interview (telephone or face-to-face) → Assessment centre → Reference checks and job offer

How employers use psychometric tests

Preference tests

In the case study in the previous section, the book publisher in Paris can use Charlotte, Tomas and Sebastian's personality profiles in two ways. The first, and most common, is to use the results to help generate questions for the next stage – the interview. The key tasks of the job that they all have applied for are:

- Networking and forging new relationships with authors and retailers.
- Setting and planning the budgets for a major department within the publishing company.

From the preference test results, the hiring manager knows that Charlotte is likely to enjoy networking and relationship building. However, given the strength of her extraversion he decides to ask Charlotte about her approach in two areas:

- He asks her how she goes about building new relationships with others and, in particular, how she balances talking with listening. This is because some people with a strong preference for extraversion can also be very talkative – possibly to the point that they can dominate conversations. It will therefore be useful to understand how she does this in practice.

Preference tests are used mainly as a tool by recruiters to shape their interview questions

- He also asks her how she manages tasks that require individual work. The budget planning process will involve spending considerable time working at a desk, without the direct involvement of others. Will Charlotte be able to work like this without being distracted by opportunities for social contact?

In the same way, the hiring manager can identify useful interview questions for Tomas and Sebastian by comparing their personality profiles with the key activities on the job description. You will notice in this example that the employer does not make assumptions about the candidates' abilities based on their personality profiles. This is because the personality questionnaire is a test of preferences and not a test of ability!

Using the test results to create shortlists of candidates

The second way employers can use preference test scores is as a direct 'cut-off', which means the hiring manager can screen out those candidates whose profiles suggest that they are unlikely to fit in well with important aspects of a job. This usually happens where there are thousands of candidates applying for only a few vacancies, or when the vacancy is for a very specific and important task that favours a particular type of personality.

For example, maintenance engineers in the nuclear industry may, in a rare emergency, have to perform critical tasks under extreme pressure in order to avert a major incident. Don't drop that spanner! We saw in Table 1.2 that one dimension of personality is known as 'emotional stability'. People who are low on this scale tend to be anxious and prone to worry. As a result, an employer filling that vacancy may decide to sift out candidates who have a low score on emotional stability.

However, for most jobs, it's hard to justify a black and white approach to using preference tests – they are used mainly as a tool that helps recruiters shape their interviews.

Ability tests

When employers use ability tests they need to select the most appropriate test or tests and then decide on an appropriate 'cut-off' score. This is the minimum score that candidates must achieve in order to pass a test. In setting a cut-off score, recruiters want to ensure that suitable candidates are retained and as many unsuitable candidates as possible as selected out. The case study below shows how employers make these decisions.

Case study

Christian works for a large government department in the UK. He is responsible for the recruitment of experienced staff within the policy and advisory unit. Christian has five vacancies for senior policy officers which he needs to fill from the 300 candidates who have applied. Like many recruiters, Christian decides to use an ability-based psychometric test early on in the selection process.

Christian examines the job description for a senior policy officer. The main responsibilities of the role are:

■ Conducting research on important social, environmental and financial issues
■ Analysing complex research data to draw conclusions
■ Writing clear and comprehensive policy documents to inform decision makers

Christian decides to use a psychometric test of verbal reasoning. These tests measure people's ability to use and reason with written words, for example, by comprehending passages of text, making inferences, and comparing arguments.

Christian wishes to use a verbal reasoning test for two reasons.

■ Firstly, the specific skills that the test measures are relevant to writing policy documents.
■ Secondly, the test also provides a measure of intelligence, which will affect the ability to conduct research and to make sense of complex results.

Christian also needs to decide on a 'cut-off score'. Remember that psychometric tests work by comparing candidates' scores with those of a comparison group. In this case, Christian is using a comparison group of managers and professionals based in the UK.

The data for the comparison group will be provided by the publisher of the test he is using. Employers can choose to set their cut-off scores at any percentile, and most organisations set a cut-off somewhere between the 30th and the 60th percentiles. Because Christian believes that good verbal reasoning is an important skill for senior policy officers, he sets the cut-off score at the 50th percentile, which is relatively high. This means that only candidates who have at least average verbal reasoning skills, in comparison with managers and professionals in the UK, will pass the test.

If we assume that almost all of Christian's 300 candidates are currently managers or professionals in the UK, we can expect about 150 of them to pass the test by scoring on, or above, the 50th percentile cut-off. In theory, all 300 candidates could pass or fail the test, although this would indicate that the pool of applicants is of an unusually high, or low, calibre.

As we have seen, recruiters often use ability and preference based psychometric tests in very different ways. Ability tests provide an absolute 'pass' or 'fail' decision, whilst preference tests are generally used in an advisory capacity.

IN A NUTSHELL

Psychometric tests are a widely used tool in employment. This chapter gave an overview of what psychometric tests are and how they are used:

- There are two main types of psychometric tests – ability tests and preference tests.
- Psychometric tests work by comparing your responses with those of other, similar people.
- For ability tests, employers use cut-off scores (a minimum percentile score) to screen out low-scoring candidates.
- For preference tests, employers most commonly use the scores to generate interview questions.

2 NUMERICAL REASONING TESTS

How good do you think you are with numbers: confident, average, panicky?

In our experience, people tend to be more nervous about numerical ability tests than any other element of a selection process. So if you are anxious about this kind of question, be reassured that you are not alone! Whether this is because of dark memories of maths classes in school or because they just seem intrinsically more daunting, the reality is that our own anxiety is often the biggest barrier to doing well in this kind of test. This chapter will try to remove some of that anxiety. Specifically, we will cover:

- Types of numerical test and what they try to measure

- Familiarisation and preparation

- Practice test items

Types of numerical test and what they measure

Businesses use a range of numerical tests to assess how able you are in dealing with different kinds of numerical information. Whether the tests are delivered online or in pencil and paper format, they have a lot in common, and this chapter is designed to help you become familiar with the most frequently used kinds of numerical items.

It's worth remembering that businesses using these tests are not usually concerned about your mathematical ability as such – they are not interested in how well you can do algebra or solve equations (unless you are applying for a role where there is a clear mathematics specialism such as engineering). What they are concerned about is your ability to use and interpret the kinds of numbers that come up in the running of a business. In practice this means:

- Identifying relevant facts from tables provided
- Working out percentages
- Working out averages
- Using basic ratios, decimals and fractions

Only a few tests nowadays – typically much older tests – use items such as arithmetic or geometric progression (i.e. can you work out the next number in a sequence of numbers). The great majority present you with work/business-related number problems. (We give you a few examples of the older-style questions at the end of this chapter.)

The most regularly used tests will present you with one of two formats:

- Table-based formats – the test will present you with information – usually in a table – and then ask you a number of questions relating to that table (or sometimes tables).
- Specific-question-based formats – these tests will ask you specific questions of the kind you are probably familiar with from school, but presented in business terminology.

Here is an example of a question-based format test question.

In an average week the production line is down for 3.5 hours. Lost production, per hour, is 1,200 units. How many units are lost in an average week?

A – 3,800   B – 4,200   C – 4,000   D – 2,400   E – 2,4000

(The answer is B: $3.5 \times 1,200 = 4,200$)

The skills needed for these questions are broadly the same; the main difference being that in the table-based formats you have to first identify the relevant information before you can calculate your answer.

This chapter concentrates on these practical, business-focused tests, which are by far the most common. For the number 'puzzle' kinds of tests, we recommend reading the 'test your own IQ' books, which still contain these kinds of items.

Practising numerical tests

Anyone can improve their ability to perform well when working on numerical problems. In everyday life we are constantly provided with opportunities to flex our numerical muscles but technology has also encouraged us to become lazy when working with numbers. How many of us bother to work out the correct change when we are shopping? Fewer and fewer I suspect because we trust computerised tills to do the work for us. How many of us bother to work out time and distance when we are driving? Again, I suspect, fewer and fewer because our car milometers and our satellite navigation systems do it for us. Refreshing your memory of the 'times tables, taking the opportunity to do basic mental arithmetic and looking for chances to estimate a numerical answer (for example, estimating roughly how much you expect your shopping to cost) are all helpful ways to get more numerically 'fit' in addition to looking at numerical test items.

Your state of mind is a big factor in doing well in this kind of test. Probably the best thing you can do to get yourself in a good state of mind is to practise! The example questions in the following sections should help you to feel more at ease with business-focused numerical tests but remember you should also take as many other opportunities to practise as you can.

GETTING FAMILIAR WITH THE TASKS

- Practise identifying relevant information from tables: if you look at the financial press, there is no shortage of projections in table form, so get used to reading them and extrapolating some of the basic facts they contain.
- Brush up your mental arithmetic: practise working out rough percentages in your head or practise roughly totting up figures and working out an average.
- Do numerical puzzles: for example Sudoku or the numerical puzzles contained in games such as 'Brain Training' on Nintendo DS.
- The BBC's Skillswise website is also a good resource for freshening up your numerical skills (www.bbc.co.uk/skillswise/).

Practice will also help you to become familiar with the kind of language used in the tests. Some tests will deliberately use business terminology in the questions. This can be off-putting if you aren't used to using this kind of language every day: terms such as 'capital ratios', 'partner equity', 'sales revenue', 'profit margin'. Don't be fazed by this terminology, it is usually easy to work out what the question is getting at without having to have an accountant's understanding of specific business terms. Again, practice and familiarity are the key.

CALCULATORS

A lot of tests allow you to use calculators if you wish and these will often be provided. If you are told that calculators are permitted then it is better to use your own – one that you are familiar with – rather than having to get to know a new instrument in 'real time' during the test! Unless you are accustomed to using complex calculators, choose a simple machine with large buttons and practise using it in advance, particularly how to work out percentages.

A lot of the more complex numerical tests actually rely on increasing the complexity of the wording in the questions to achieve a higher difficulty level. Now, it is arguable whether this is a real test of numerical ability. However, it does mean that you need to read the questions very carefully to make sure you understand what is being asked. If you are puzzled, looking at the multiple choice answers will give you a clue. For example, are the possible answers all percentages; are they all numbers in the thousands; are they all decimals? Knowing this can often help you to interpret even quite verbally complex questions.

Tips for top scores

In the following sections we give you a number of examples of different formats to try out, together with correct answers (at the end of the chapter) and the steps needed to get to the right answer. We have also rated the questions as easy, moderate or hard. This will help you to get a sense of the questions or question formats you find easiest or most difficult and plan your practice accordingly.

Assess the information provided

For table-based questions, look at the tables before you start on each question. Getting a sense of the information they are giving you (or not giving you) will make it easier to understand the questions. For example, if you have looked through the tables and can see that the information relates to sales figures (in millions) and profitability (in £ per item sold), this will enable you to interpret each question more easily and to head more quickly for the table that contains the information you need to work out the answer.

Get a sense of the questions or question formats you find easiest or most difficult and plan your practice accordingly

It is all too easy to get flustered when faced by a page of tables; don't rush, give yourself some time to navigate your way around the information and to understand the format the tables are using. For example, in business tables it is very common to keep the information in the columns and rows as simple as possible by putting a heading on the column explaining that the numbers in the tables are in thousands ('000') in millions ('000,000') or that they refer to percentages. Give yourself time to read these headings so that you can make sure you are using the right information in your calculations.

Visualise the question

People sometimes find it difficult to deal with the 'abstract' nature of numbers – particularly large numbers – saying things like 'the numbers all just get jumbled up in my head' or 'half way through the calculation I just lost track of what I was doing'. Turning numbers into something more concrete is one way of reducing this problem. You may remember this technique from school, where turning 'a' 'b' or 'x' and 'y' into apples or bananas seemed to make the problem less daunting!

For some people, it also helps to 'visualise' the question rather than just think about the numbers in front of you. So, for example, in the table in Section A (page 29) – Crowbridge Hotel room figures – imagine the hotel, picture it in your mind. The double rooms are probably bigger than the single rooms; perhaps the suites – there are only eight of them – are all on the top floor. Doing this helps to make the questions more practical and less abstract, and a lot of people find this helpful.

Now try the same technique for the information in the Adams Heaters example on p.31.

Remember there is no 'one right way' of doing this, you need to try it out and see if it helps. Here is our 'visualised' response to the information in the Adams Heaters tables.

- Perhaps the 20 watt heaters are about the size of a matchbox.
- Perhaps the 1 kilowatt heaters are about the size of a suitcase.
- They sell a lot of the 120 watt heaters so perhaps they have better packaging?
- They don't sell many of the 40 watt heaters so perhaps it is an old model?

The idea, remember, is to make the information less abstract – not just numbers on a page – and more real. For people who are not particularly confident in working with numbers this helps to 'de-mystify' this kind of question.

Using these tips will help you in two ways. Firstly, of course, we know that they work and will help you to find the right answers more quickly and with greater confidence. Secondly, simply having a method – a set of tools that you can easily use – is often the crucial difference between focused problem solving and increasingly anxious floundering. When you do get stuck on a question, as everyone does from time to time, it really helps to have a systematic approach to get you back on track. Both of these tips give you that clear 'back to first principles' approach.

As you work through the practice examples on the following pages make use of these tips as often as you can. As you gain in experience, notice how you start to apply the techniques without having to consciously 'use' them. The easier this becomes, the more fluent you will be in working through each type of question. Ultimately this means that you will have time to answer more questions and increase your score.

PRACTICE QUESTIONS

(answers can be found at the end of the chapter on page 41)

A. Table-based formats (easy)

Crowbridge Hotel room figures 2010

Type of room	Number of rooms available	Average number of days per year each room occupied
Single rooms	25	245
Double rooms	20	260
Family rooms (four beds)	20	310
Suites (four beds)	8	190

1. On average, how many days in the year were the family rooms occupied?

   A – 300   B – 260   C – 390   D – 310   E – 245

2. Excluding suites, how many rooms are available in the hotel?

   A – 48   B – 65   C – 60   D – 75   E – 55

3. If every family room held its maximum number of occupants, how many people could the hotel accommodate in family rooms on any given night?

   A – 80   B – 32   C – 88   D – 100   E – Can't say

4. Assuming that the average occupancy applies to every room, which type of room had the greatest total number of occupied days?

   A – Double   B – Single   C – Family   D – Suite   E – Can't say

5. To the nearest whole number, what percentage of the hotels rooms is made up of family rooms?

   A – 20%   B – 25%   C – 30%   D – 27%   E – 33%

Crowbridge River Ferry Statistics

Season	Number of crossings per day	Average number of passengers per crossing
Spring	20	12
Summer	24	18
Autumn	18	12
Winter	16	10

6. In spring, how many passengers – on average – use the ferry each day?

   A – 12   B – 120   C – 240   D – 220   E – 180

7. Across all seasons, what is the average number of passengers per crossing?

   A – 12   B – 13   C – 18   D – 16   E – Can't say

8. If each passenger is charged £3.00 to use the ferry, what is the average revenue per day in the winter season?

   A – £480   B – £560   C – £460   D – £510   E – £490

9. On average, how many more passengers per day use the ferry in the spring + summer seasons as compared with the autumn + winter seasons?

   A – 12   B – 10   C – 8   D – 6   E – Can't say

10. Assuming there are 90 days in each season, what is the total number of crossings each year?

   A – 6800   B – 6950   C – 7200   D – 7250   E – 7020

B. Table-based formats (easy/moderate)

Adams Heaters: sales figures for 2010

Heater type	Profit per heater
20 W	£5.00
40 W	£5.00
80 W	£4.00
120 W	£3.50
1 kW	£7.50

Sales in 000s of units – 2010

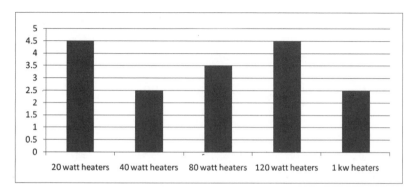

Note, in the following questions you might have to use information from either the table or the figure or both kinds of information.

1. **How much total profit was generated by 1 kilowatt heaters?**

   A – £18,750   B – £25,000   C – £2,500   D – £17,500   E – £19,750

2. **Which type of heater generated the greatest total profit?**

   A – 20 watt   B – 40 watt   C – 80 watt   D – 120 watt   E – 1 kilowatt

3. **If the sales of 1 kilowatt heaters were doubled, how much more profit would they make than the current sales of 80 watt heaters?**

   A – £6,500   B – £32,000   C – £25,500   D – £22,250   E – £23,500

4. What is the average profitability across all the heater types?

    A – £4.50   B – £5.00   C – £4.25   D – £6.00   E – £6.25

5. If 1 kilowatt heaters sold 20% less than they currently do, what would
    the total sales of 40 watt heaters have to be to achieve the same overall
    profit?

    A – 750   B – 3,000   C – 3,250   D – 3,750   E – 4,750

6. If improved production methods enabled the profitability of 2 watt
    heaters to be raised to £6.00 per unit, and this was sustained for 6
    months of next year (2011), what percentage of total profitability for
    2011 would be accounted for by 2 watt heaters?

    A – 20%   B – 24%   C – 32%   D – 15%   E – Can't say

C. Table-based formats (moderate/hard)

Vale Foods Ltd – Year on year sales (millions of units)

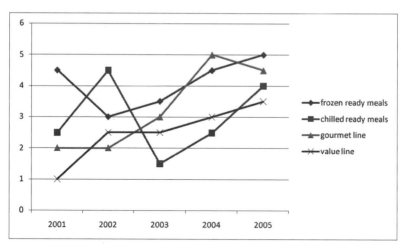

Production capacity in 2005

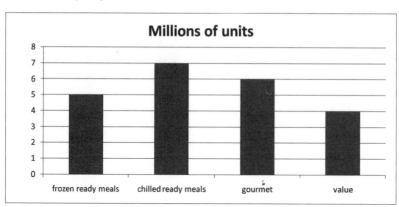

1. **Which was the most profitable product line in 2003?**

   A – Frozen   B – Chilled   C – Can't say D – Gourmet   E – Value

2. **Across all product lines, what was the difference between total sales in 2001 and 2002?**

   A – 5 million B – 3 million   C – 1.5 million   D – 2 million   E – 1 million

3. Across the 5 years for which information is available, which product has the highest sales?

    A – Value   B – Can't say   C – Chilled   D – Frozen   E – Gourmet

4. In 2005, what is the total excess of production over sales?

    A – 6 million   B – 8 million   C – 5 million   D – Can't say   E – 4 million

5. Assuming production capacity was the same as in 2005, what percentage of production capacity for the chilled ready meals line – to the nearest whole number – was sold in 2002?

    A – 64%   B – 70%   C – 62%   D – 68%   E – 69%

6. If production capacity for frozen meals was cut by a half and production capacity for gourmet meals was cut by a third, by what amount would total capacity exceed total sales in 2005?

    A – 1 million   B – 500,000   C – 750,000   D – 1.5 million E – 250,000

7. If the average annual sales growth for the value line between 2001 and 2005 was projected ahead to 2006, by what percentage would production capacity for the value line have to increase (to the nearest whole number)?

    A – 12%   B – 5%   C – 3%   D – 7%   E – 2%

D. Specific-question-based formats

(easy)

1. How many employees, at a recruitment cost of £3,000 each, can be hired if the recruitment budget is £261,000?

   A – 76   B – 87   C – 78   D – 74   E – 82

2. If sales of toys grew by 26% this year, from last year's figure of 820,000, what is the figure for this year's sales?

   A – 1,033,200   B – 1,133,200   C – 1,230,000
   D – 1,123,000   E – 1,280,300

3. Productivity for the last 5 years has been 78%, 74%, 81%, 80% and 84%. What has been the average productivity over this period?

   A – 81%   B – 78.9%   C – 80.5 %   D – 79.9%   E – 79.4%

4. There are 7 people working in your team; in total they worked for 270.9 hours last week. What was the average number of hours worked per person?

   A – 37.8 hours   B – 38.7 hours   C – 38 hours
   D – 36.8 hours   E – 38.6 hours

5. Your Band 1 staff earn on average 34% more than your Band 2 staff. If the average salary for Band 2 staff is £31,000, what is the average salary of a Band 1 employee?

   A – £40,450   B – £41,750   C – £40,750   D – £41,540   E – £41,175

E. Specific-question-based formats

(moderate)

1. Your factory has three production lines – A, B and C – producing 104, 127 and 94 units per hour, respectively. In an 8-hour shift how many more units will lines A and B combined produce compared with line C?

   A – 1,750   B – 1,096   C – 1,607   D – 1,960   E – 1,069

2. The average age of employees in your business is 38.5 years. The average age for men is 40.5 years; what is the average age for women?

   A – 38 years   B – 36.5 years   C – 35.5 years
   D – 37 years   E – Can't say

3. Anderson, Hilton and Weston are the three partners in a firm of solicitors, owning 40%, 35% and 25% of the equity in the business, respectively. Profits are divided up in proportion to each partner's equity in the business. If the business makes a profit of £475,600 then how much more will Hilton receive compared with Weston?

   A – £43,750   B – £47,560   C – £35,500   D – £39,470   E – Can't say

4. Your business currently borrows £350,000 at an annual interest rate of 6% on the first £200,000 and 7.5% on the remainder. You have the opportunity to pay off this debt by selling one of your retail units although you will be selling the unit at a loss of £58,000. How many years will it take for the saving in interest to cover the loss (to the nearest decimal place)?

   A – 2 years   B – 2.2 years   C – 2.7 years   D – 3.1 years   E – 2.5 years

5. The annual profits made by two London stores are £2,340,000 for the Oxford Street branch and £1,920,000 for the Strand branch. These profits are spread equally across all 12 months of the year. Both stores need to be refurbished; this will involve closing them for a period. If Oxford Street is closed for 2.5 months and the Strand is closed for 1.5 months, how much profit will be lost?

   A – £727,500 B – £750,000 C – £687,500 D – £770,500 E – £690,500

F. Specific-question-based formats

(hard)

1. On a turnover of £8.5 million, the gross profit made by your business is £2.7 million. From this figure must be taken overhead costs of £1,425,000 to arrive at net profit. What is the net profit to turnover ratio?

   A – 17.5%   B – 15.5%   C – 15%   D – 16.5%   E – 16%

2. In your sales team Andy sells 43 units per month, Ajaz sells 52 units per month and Sue sells 62 units per month: they offer discounts of £18, £23 and £21, respectively, per unit they sell. The total value (undiscounted) of units sold by the three in a month is £25,905. In a full year, by how much will the amount of Ajaz's and Sue's discount together exceed Andy's?

   A – £25,600   B – £20,688   C – £21,645   D – £22,555   E – £20,750

3. The total spend of the marketing department of your firm last year was 1.6 million on advertising, 0.8 million on public relations, 0.3 million on brochures and 0.7 million on corporate events. The marketing budget represents 13% of the firm's turnover. If the marketing budget for last year was underspent by 20%, what was the firm's turnover to the nearest million?

   A – 30 million B – 34 million   C – 38 million D – 33 million   E – 31 million

4. Every year your business sets aside £750,000 to cover legal costs. The money is spent with three separate law firms: Williams Partners (Litigation), Singh Partners (Employment Law) and Brace Brothers (Contract Law) in the proportion 5:3:2, respectively. Brace Brothers is proposing to increase its charges by 15%, while Singh Partners is proposing to reduce its by 5%. In total, how much money would you save by giving your contract law business to Singh Partners?

   A – £30,000   B – £18,750   C – £25,000   D – £35,500   E – £27,550

G. Other numerical formats

We mentioned at the start of this chapter that some, usually older, tests make use of items that are based on 'pure' numerical reasoning. You are much less likely to run across this kind of item but just so that you recognise them if they do come up, this section gives them some brief coverage.

You will occasionally see tests that are essentially about basic arithmetic; the format is usually as follows:

$56 - 9 = 7 + ?$	Answer = 40
$18 \times 5 = 9 \times ?$	Answer = 10
$5 \times 13 + 27 = 11 \times 8 + ?$	Answer = 4
$6.3 \times 2.9 \times 4.8 = ?$	Answer = 87.69
$4 \times ? = 47 + 9 \times 8$	Answer = 112

There is no real trick to items like this: it is simply a matter of working through the calculation, making sure you are accurate about whether you are adding, subtracting, multiplying or dividing to work out the unknown number. Such tests often don't allow you to use a calculator, so make sure your long division and long multiplication are up to scratch!

Another category of test – again asking you to identify a missing number – is based on you having to identify the rule that lets you predict the missing number. Here are some examples:

6	9	12	15	18	?

This is a simple arithmetic progression: you get the next number by adding 3 each time so the missing value is 21. So the rule here is 'add 3'. Here are some more examples of arithmetic progressions:

1.	225	200	175	150	?
2.	9	19	28	36	?
3.	13	20	27	34	?

Slightly more complex are geometric progressions where you have to multiply or divide to get the next number: again, the trick is to work out the rule that lets you predict the missing value. Here are some examples:

4. 3   9   27   81   ?

5. 4   16   256   ?

6. 480   120   30   7.5   ?

Another category of test is the number 'puzzle' kind of test. These are usually just a combination of arithmetic and/or geometric progressions – so again the issue is to find the rule that is being applied. Some of the formats in which these tests are presented can be quite novel, however. It is not possible to cover every variation you might encounter but here are some representative examples:

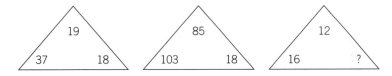

Here the rule is to take the smaller from the larger number on the left in each triangle, to get the number on the bottom right in each triangle. The answer is 4. Remember that the rule will probably change from item to item so you will need to work it out each time. Here are some more examples:

7.

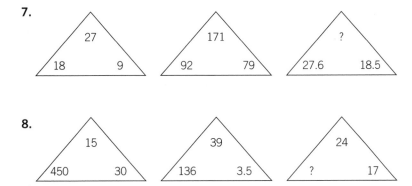

8.

A final format you might see is a 'puzzle' presented in table format as follows:

2	4	6
5	7	9
8	10	?

Here, the rule is that numbers increase by 2 from left to right and by three from top to bottom. In this case it doesn't matter which rule you apply, you still get the answer 12. As before, however, the rule will usually change from item to item so you need to work it out each time. Here are some more examples:

9.

2	4	6
5	7	9
7	11	?

10.

7	10	70
8	8	64
4	13	?

There are so many different variations on this theme that it is not possible to cover all of them here. For this general kind of item, however, a good tip is to focus on the two columns and the two rows in each grid where you have complete information in order to work out the rule.

Numerical Tests – Answers

A.1 **D – 310 days** (This is simply a matter of reading the right line in the table; namely that the family rooms were occupied for an average of 310 days.)

A.2 **B – 65** (Adding the numbers in column one but excluding the 8 for suites to get the total.)

A.3 **A – 80** (20 family rooms × 4 possible occupants.)

A.4 **C – Family room** (note that they are asking about the *type* of room). To get total occupancy you multiply column one by column two for each type of room thus:

Single   25 × 245 = 6,125
Double   20 × 260 = 5,200
Family   20 × 310 = 6,200
Suite   8 × 190 = 1,520

A.5 **D – 27%** (Calculated by dividing the number of family rooms (20) by the total number of rooms (73) and multiplying by 100. The accurate answer is 27.3972%, but they only want it to the nearest whole number!)

A.6 **C – 240** (The calculation is simply the number of crossings per day in spring(20) multiplied by the average number of passengers per crossing in spring(12): the only thing to watch out for is to notice that they are asking for passengers per day not per crossing.)

A.7 **B – 13** (The calculation is to add the average number of passengers per crossing across all seasons (12+18+12+10) and then divide by 4 to get the answer)

A.8 **A – £480** (Simply 16 x 10 to give the average number of passengers per day in winter, multiplied by £3.00 to give the revenue.)

A.9 **C – 8** (12+10 subtracted from 12+18.)

A.10 E – 7020 (You need to multiply each of the seasonal crossings per day by 90 and then add these together)

B.1 A – £18,750 (The answer is simply the profit per 1 kilowatt heater (£7.50 from the first table) multiplied by the number of units sold (2,500 from the first figure) to get the answer.)

B.2 A – 20 watt heater (The answer again is simply the profit per heater multiplied by the number sold and then looking for the highest figure. However, you can save some time here by estimating. Looking at the numbers, you should be able to estimate that the 20 watt and 1 kilowatt heaters are the only real contenders; the 40 watt heater doesn't sell enough, the 80 watt heater sells less and is less profitable and the 120 watt has the same volume as the 20 watt but is much less profitable. The complete total profit table is as follows:

20 watt	£22,500
40 watt	£12,500
80 watt	£14,000
120 watt	£15,750
1 kW	£18,750

So the answer is the 20 watt heater with a total profit of £22,500.)

B.3 E – £23,500 (You have probably done a lot of this calculation already in answering question B2. Current total profit for 80 watt heaters is £14,000 (3,500 × £4); doubling the current total profit of 1 kilowatt heaters is £37,500 (2,500 × £7.5 × 2) and then subtracting one from the other to get the answer.)

B.4 B – £5.00 (This is an easy question so don't make it more complicated; they are asking about profit per *type* of heater so it is simply the average of the figures in the first table.)

B.5 C – 3,250 (Now this looks nasty but it's not that bad. 1 kilowatt heaters currently sell 2,500 units; 20% less than this is 2,000. So, if you are selling 500 less of them at £7.50 each you have a profit shortfall of

£3,750 (500 × £7.5). So, how many more of the 40 watt heaters – at a profit of £5.00 each – do you have to sell to make up the difference? Simply 3,750 divided by 5 which equals 750, but this is not the answer! They ask for the *total* sales of 40 watt heaters, not additional sales, so you have to add 750 to the current sales (2,500) to get the answer. See what we mean about reading the question carefully?)

B.6 **E – Can't say** (You are not given sales figures for next year so you can't calculate total profitability, so you can't say what percentage the profit for 20 watt heaters would account for. To make this calculation possible they would either have had to give you projected sales figures for 2011, or told you to assume the same sales figures as the current year. They didn't, so you can't say!)

C.1   **C – Can't say** (They do not give you any information about profitability, only about sales.)

C.2   **D – 2 million** (Simply calculated by adding up the sales figures for 2001 (1 + 2 + 2.5 + 4.5 = 10), adding up the sales figures for 2002 (2 + 2.5 + 3 + 4.5 = 12) and taking one from the other to get the answer.)

C.3   **D – Frozen** (Calculated by adding the sales figures for each product for each year as follows:

Frozen   =   20.5 million
Chilled   =   15 million
Gourmet   =   16.5 million
Value   =   12.5 million)

C.4   **C – 5 million** (Calculated by comparing the two graphs and noting that:

Frozen   production and sales are the same
Chilled   production exceeds sales by 3 million
Gourmet   production exceeds sales by 1.5 million
Value   production exceeds sales by 0.5 million

Giving an excess of 5 million in total.)

C.5   **A – 64%** (64.28 to be accurate; calculated by assuming that production capacity in 2002 was 7 million (they tell you to assume this), of which 4.5 million was sold, so 4.5 divided by 7 $\times$ 100 = 64)

C.6   **B – 500,000** (Calculated as follows: cutting frozen meals capacity by half means production capacity is now 2.5 million (down from 5 million), cutting gourmet meals capacity by a third means production capacity is now 4 million (down from 6 million). So, 4.5 million has been cut from production capacity; 2005 capacity is currently 22 million; take away 4.5 million and you are left with a total production capacity of 17.5 million. Total sales in 2005 are 17 million, so capacity exceeds sales by 500,000!)

C.7   **C – 3%** (Worked out as follows: first you need to know the average sales growth for the value line, like this:

2001–2002   growth = 1.5 million
2002–2003   growth = 0
2003–2004   growth = 0.5 million
2004–2005   growth = 0.5 million

Add up (to get 2.5 million) and divide by 4 to get an average sales growth of 0.625 million per year. If you now add this to the 2005 figure (3.5 million) you get a projected figure for 2006 of 4.125 million. So how much more is this than the current production capacity of 4 million? Time for percentages again: 4 million divided by 4.125 million × 100 = 96.96% (rounded up to 97%). This means you can currently only produce 97% of what you predict will be needed in 2006, so production capacity has to increase by 3%.)

D.1   **B – 87** (The calculation is 261,000 divided by 3,000.)

D.2   **A – 1,033,200** (The calculation is 820,000 divided by 100 × 26 added to the original 820,000.)

D.3   **E – 79.4%** (The calculation is 78 + 74 + 81 + 80 + 84 divided by 5.)

D.4   **B – 38.7 hours** (The calculation is 270.9 divided by 7.)

D.5   **D – £41,540** (The calculation is 31,000 divided by 100, multiplied by 34, added to the original 31,000.)

E.1   **B – 1096** (The calculation is (104 × 8) + (127 × 8) minus (94 × 8).)

E.2   **E – Can't say** (Without knowing the numbers of male and female employees there is no way of calculating a precise answer. You can estimate that the average age of women must be less than 38.5 years – given that men have a higher average age – but you can't put a figure on it.)

E.3   **B – £47,560** (The calculation is 35% of £475,600 (= 166,460) minus

25% of £475,600 (= 118,900) to give a difference of £47,560. This is actually a straightforward percentages question but it is made to appear more complicated by the use of terms like 'equity' and by the option of a 'Can't say' answer. The moral of the tale is look for the simple route to the answer.)

E.4   E – 2.5 years (The calculation is first, the annual cost of borrowing, which is 6% of 200,000 plus 7.5% of 150,000 (12,000 + 11,250) to get a total cost of borrowing of £23,250. Divide this into 58,000 to see how long it will take to get your money back. The accurate answer is 2.4946 years but the question only asks for accuracy to one decimal place.)

E.5   A – £727,500 (The calculation is to work out the monthly profitability of each store (simply dividing the annual profit by 12) then multiply the monthly profit by the number of months the store will be closed as follows. Monthly profitability of Oxford Street is £195,000 × 2.5 months closed, added to the monthly profitability of the Strand, which is £160,000 × 1.5 months closed to get the answer.)

F.1   C – 15% (The calculation is first to work out net profit (simply 2,700,000 minus 1,425,000 = 1,275,000) and then to present this number as a percentage of 8.5 million. (1,275,000 divided by 8,500,000 × 100) The only complication here is the slightly intimidating language.)

F.2   B – £20,688 (The calculation is the number of units sold × the discount value for each person, multiplied by 12 to get the total for each person for a year. It is then simply a matter of adding Ajaz's and Sue's totals together and subtracting the total for Andy to get the answer. The challenge with this question is too much information: it tempts you to work out the sale price of each unit through the information given in the second sentence but this information is redundant! You can calculate the answer through the very complicated route of working out the undiscounted value of each person's sales, then removing the discount, but you don't need to do this. A good example of where a couple of minutes given to understanding the gist of the question can save you a lot of calculator time!)

F.3 **D – 33 million** (The calculation is first to get the total marketing spend (1.6 + 0.8 + 0.3 + 0.7 = 3.4 million), this represents 80% of the marketing budget so the total marketing budget would have been 3.4 million divided by 80 × 100 = 4,250,000. This number in turn is 13% of turnover so total turnover will be 4,250,000 divided by 13 × 100. The accurate answer is 32,692,307 but the question only asks for the nearest million.)

F.4 **A – £30,000** (The calculation is first to work out the amount spent with each law firm. To do this, translate proportions into percentages thus: 5 + 3 + 2 = 10, so Williams has 5 tenths of the budget (50%), Singh has 3 tenths (30%) and Brace has 2 tenths (20%). As percentages of the total budget this equates to:

Williams	=	£375,000
Singh	=	£225,000
Brace	=	£150,000

From this basis you can work out what the proposed increases and decreases mean if you apportion work as you do currently, so your costs will be £11,250 less with Singh but £22,500 more with Brace. The secret here is to recognise that one option leads to an increase in cost while the other leads to a reduction and you must put the two together to get the difference or total saving. If things stay the same, Singh will be charging you £11,250 less but Brace will be charging you £22,500 more, in total an increase of £11,250. By moving the contract business to Singh and away from Brace you will be getting a 5% discount on a new total of £375,000 which equals £18,750 less. Thus the total difference (saving) is £18,750 + £11,250 = £30,000 less compared with what you would have had to spend otherwise.)

G.1 **125** (The rule is subtract 25.)

G.2 **43** (The rule is add 1 less each time: 10, 9, 8, 7, 6.)

G.3 **41** (The rule is add 7.)

G.4 **243** (The rule is multiply by 3.)

G.5 **65,536** (The rule is multiply each number by itself.)

G.6 **1.875** (The rule is divide by 4.)

G.7 **46.1** (Here the rule is to add the two lower numbers in each triangle to get the number at the apex.)

G.8 **408** (Here the rule is to multiply the two numbers on the right in each triangle to get the number on the bottom left.)

G.9 **15** (Here the rule is simply to add up the top two numbers in each column to get the bottom number.)

G.10 **52** (Here the rule is to multiply the first two numbers in each row to get the third number.)

IN A NUTSHELL

Numerical reasoning tests are used to measure your ability to interpret the kinds of number work that you would encounter in the running of a business.

- Practise using numerical information; for example, increase your familiarity with extracting information from tables. For table based questions, give yourself a minute to familiarise yourself with the information they contain.
- Make sure you can work out percentages and brush up on your long division and long multiplication; get to know and trust your calculator.
- Read the questions carefully, don't do calculations that you don't have to!
- Make full use of the practice items you will be given at the start of any test; make sure you understand the format.
- Don't be fazed by business language and terminology; if you have found any of the language in the example questions intimidating, then make time during your preparation to look up specific words or practise reading business-related material.

3 VERBAL REASONING TESTS

Employers will often want to make an assessment of prospective employees' reasoning skills, and verbal reasoning tests are the most common way that they try to do this. In this chapter we will:

- Explain what the commonly used tests are trying to measure

- Familiarise you with different response formats

- Give you the opportunity to practise verbal reasoning tests

What verbal reasoning tests measure

Verbal tests are designed to assess how well you use vocabulary, solve problems, reason and apply logic using words. Sometimes they are described as 'logical reasoning' or 'critical thinking' tests but they all depend on use and understanding of words to assess your thinking. As you can probably tell from this mixture of abilities, verbally based tests are often trying to measure more than one thing at the same time. Essentially, they usually try to measure the following aspects of your verbal ability, sometimes in combination and sometimes separately:

- **Comprehension** – can you read a short passage and accurately find required information or facts within it?
- **Logic and logical relationships** – can you deduce a conclusion based on the information you are given?
- **Word meaning/vocabulary** – do you understand the precise meaning of words, can you select substitute words that mean the same thing?

By far the most common form of these tests is to present you with a passage of information and then to ask you a number of questions about it; either comprehension questions or logic questions and sometimes a combination of the two. As before, a potential employer is much less interested in your literary skills – unless you are applying for a specific role which involves writing, such as journalism – and much more interested in whether you can understand and extract the relevant information from written material.

Employers are interested in whether you can understand and extract relevant information from written material

We will concentrate on giving you examples of these most commonly used test formats.

Once again, preparation, practice and familiarity are important factors in doing well in verbal tests. Take advantage of the sample items on test publishers' websites (see Chapter 8). People vary a great deal in terms of how much time they spend reading – at work or as a leisure activity. There is no doubt that your confidence and comfort in reading is a big factor in doing well in such tests, so, if you do not read a great deal, additional practice here is likely to pay off.

Response formats

All the verbal tests you encounter will ask you to respond in multiple choice format, selecting the option that you think is correct. The most common format is to ask you to read a short passage of information and then answer questions based on the information.

Comprehension tests

In comprehension tests, i.e. finding the right information in the passage, you will be given the usual choice of answers, usually between three and five, and asked to select the one you think is most accurate.

Logic tests

In logic tests you will be asked to look at a statement they give you and to respond:

- **True** – if you think the statement is correct and/or follows logically from the information given.
- **False** – if you think the statement is incorrect or does not follow on logically from the information given.
- **Can't say** – if you can't tell whether the statement is correct or otherwise based on the information given.

STICK TO THE GIVEN FACTS

Most verbal tests will warn you to base your answers on the information given and not on your own knowledge or opinions about the subject matter of the passage. So, for example, you might be asked to read a passage about a subject on which you are well informed, having your own views and knowledge; you must base your answers on the information given and not on your own opinions even if, factually, your view is more accurate.

Word meaning tests

In word meaning tests you will usually be asked to:

- **Replace words** – by selecting an alternative word from a list.
- **Identify synonyms and antonyms** – words that mean the same or opposite of a given word, again selected from a list of alternatives.

You might also – increasingly rarely these days – come across old-fashioned IQ type verbal items such as:

Dog is to puppy as cat is to:

☐ Small
☐ Furry
☐ Kitten
☐ Pet
☐ Parent

These are now so uncommon that we won't cover them here but plenty of items of this kind are available online if you want to explore them. Chapter 8 provides some references to this kind of material.

Tips for top scores

- Practise – use the example items to improve your speed at pulling out key information.
- Read questions very carefully; make sure you understand what is being asked for.
- If you do not read a great deal, then set aside time for reading to increase the speed at which you can spot relevant information.
- Improving your 'lexicon' of word meanings can take time; again, reading more will help but challenge yourself by reading material where you will encounter words that are unfamiliar and that you will need to look up.

PRACTICE QUESTIONS

(answers can be found at the end of the chapter on page 72)

The following sections have a number of examples of different formats to try out, together with correct answers and the logic used to get to the right answer. We have rated the questions as easy, moderate or hard. This will help you to get a sense of which questions or question formats you find easiest or most difficult so that you can plan your practice accordingly.

In turn, the practice examples will include:

■ Comprehension questions – finding information in a passage of writing
■ Logic questions – drawing conclusions about what is correct or incorrect based on information given
■ Word meaning/vocabulary

Comprehension (easy)

Example A

Read the passage below and then answer the following questions:

'These days, most areas of science have become so specialised that it is no longer possible to be an "all rounder". Our Victorian predecessors had the luxury of being able to span physics, chemistry and the natural sciences and develop a respectable knowledge across a number of disciplines. For example, Lord Kelvin made vital contributions to physics, engineering and geology; Sir Francis Galton made important contributions to meteorology, psychology and biology. Such polymaths were relatively common in the 19th century but are hard to find now.'

1. **Which of these disciplines is not mentioned in the passage?**

   a. Biology
   b. Astronomy
   c. Physics
   d. Chemistry
   e. Natural sciences

2. **Which one of these statements most accurately reflects the key points of the passage?**

   a. Victorians were great scientists
   b. It is important to know more than one science
   c. Victorian scientists were greatly respected
   d. It is harder now to be a scientific generalist than it was in the past
   e. Science is too specialised

3. **For which one of the following reasons is it harder to find polymaths now?**

   a. There was more time to study in the 19th century
   b. People such as Lord Kelvin had wider interests
   c. Individual sciences have become much more specialised
   d. People are less interested in science now
   e. Science used to be taught better

Example B

Read the passage below and then answer the following questions:

'Few people can afford to be complacent about their pensions in the current situation, particularly those of us depending on private pensions. The poor performance of the stock market over the last 10 years means that pension funds have not delivered their promised rates of return and for a lot of us this means substantially less income to see us through retirement. Most independent pensions advisers are saying that private pensions are underinvested by about 40%, meaning that the average saver needs to be investing £5,000 more each year than they currently do if they want to protect their retirement income. Whether you are planning to buy an annuity or whether you have other plans for investing your pension pot on retirement, chances are that it will not deliver what you expect.'

1. **Which one of the following reasons best explains why pension funds have underperformed?**

    a. Pension investors have been too cautious
    b. People are not listening to their independent financial advisers
    c. Private pensions are not as good as state pensions
    d. People cannot afford to invest enough
    e. The stock market has performed poorly

2. **Which one of these sentences most accurately paraphrases the first sentence in the passage?**

    a. Currently, people with private pensions are especially at risk if they are too complacent
    b. All pensioners need to be more vigilant about future earnings
    c. Poor stock market performance puts us all at risk
    d. People with private pensions will have problems buying annuities
    e. It is dangerous to depend on private pensions

3. **Which one of these headlines most accurately summarises the content of the passage?**

    a. 'Pensions funds are in trouble'
    b. 'Pensions advisers warn of need for more investment'
    c. 'Annuities are 40% down on predictions'
    d. 'Stock market still down after 10 years'
    e. 'Bad time to invest in pensions'

Comprehension (moderate/hard)

Example C

Read the passage below and then answer the following questions:

'Everyone is capable of creativity and innovation. Although it comes more easily to some than others – dependent on personality, aptitude and motivation – we all have brains that are evolved for creative problem solving. So why don't we all get the chance? Some of the answer lies in the stereotypes we have of ourselves or our roles, but what is R&D if not a creative activity; what is enterprise if not a creative activity; what is writing just a memo if not a creative activity? All these are about making something, whether it is a compound, a business or an idea. The environment and the climate that we work in are key determinants of how much of our creativity we bring to work. Do we work in a highly controlling environment where analysis overrides original thinking? Are we managed in a way that focuses on control, metrics and short term deliverables rather than on broader, more open ended thinking? Does our business climate reward systematisation more than speculation? An unsupportive creativity climate makes it all the more likely that we will save our moments of inspiration for the weekend!'

1. **Which pair of statements best describe reasons for a lack of creativity?**

    a. Everyone can be creative + an unsupportive creativity climate
    b. Our stereotypes of ourselves + our brains are evolved to be creative
    c. A highly controlling environment + management focused on the short term
    d. Too much analysis + everyone is capable of innovation

2. **According to the information provided, why does creativity come more easily to some people than to others?**

    a. We have brains evolved for problem solving
    b. It depends on personality, aptitude and motivation
    c. Businesses focus on short-term deliverables
    d. Not everyone gets the chance

3. **Which of the following phrases best captures the meaning of the phrase '*we will save our moments of inspiration for the weekend*' at the end of the passage?**

    a. People tend to be more creative in their own time
    b. Businesses miss an opportunity if they don't support creativity
    c. People resent being controlled
    d. Creativity depends on a lot of different factors

4. **Which of the following statements is closest in meaning to the phrase '*The environment and the climate that we work in are key determinants of how much of our creativity we bring to work.*'**

    a. How we are feeling makes a difference to how creative we are
    b. Company culture and the way we are managed are important influences on our creativity at work
    c. Most of us are more creative at home than we are at work
    d. If we are determined we can all overcome barriers to creativity

Example D

Read the following passage then answer the questions:

'Arguments in health economics are always challenging ones; the fundamental difficulty of aligning scarce resources with apparently infinite demand means that prioritising – in itself problematic and subject to multiple sources of influence – becomes as much a political as a scientific or strictly rational process. Health economists find relatively little difficulty in calculating return on investment for a particular therapeutic intervention (for example in terms of speed of recovery), or in estimating average individual benefit in terms of quality of life or extended life expectancy, but find it much more difficult to provide an "economic" answer as to the value of newer therapeutic options such as fertility treatment where the payoff is hard to define in individual or societal terms but is, rather, a matter of personal well-being or even human rights. As a result, the economic arguments for supporting or proscribing a therapy will never be the only consideration when it comes to making difficult decisions about how to ration health care.'

1. **Which of these statements best explains why health economics decisions are difficult?**

   a. Political factors are as important as economic ones
   b. Demand for treatment exceeds supply
   c. New therapies are always being developed
   d. There are a wide range of factors that have to be considered

2. **Which of these sentences would best replace the final sentence in the passage?**

   a. As a result difficult decisions about health care will always involve a lot of factors
   b. As a result economics will be only one of the factors influencing health care decisions
   c. As a result decisions about how to ration health care will always be difficult
   d. As a result there are always economic arguments for supporting or proscribing a particular therapy

3. Which of these phrases best summarises the content of the passage?

    a.   Some therapies, such as fertility treatment, are harder to justify than others

    b.   Health economists find it difficult to take account of factors such as personal well-being

    c.   The economic case is only part of the argument when it comes to decisions about health care

    d.   Tangible benefits such as increased life expectancy should get a higher priority when it comes to decisions about health care

4. Which of these statements is factually accurate based on the information in the passage?

    a.   Decisions about how to prioritise are subject to political influence

    b.   It is difficult to calculate return on investment for most therapies

    c.   Average extended life expectancy is the most frequently used measure of patient benefit

    d.   Newer therapies will inevitably take time to prove their value

Logic and logical relationships (easy)

In these questions, read the passage provided and then decide whether each of the statements following the passage is:

- **True** – if you think the statement is correct and/or follows logically from the information given.
- **False** – if you think the statement is incorrect or does not follow on logically from the information given.
- **Can't say** – if you can't tell whether the statement is correct or otherwise based on the information given.

Example E

'Situated close to the river Thames, the Tower of London is home to the Crown Jewels and one of the most famous castles in England. Founded by William the Conqueror in about 1070, the Tower has been at the centre of English history for almost 1,000 years; over this period it has served as a fortress, a royal palace, a prison and an armoury. William's first construction on the site would have been a relatively hastily erected building of timber and stone; the White Tower – the main central keep – was started in 1078, taking about 10 years to build, and has been significantly added to and improved since.'

For each statement answer A – True; B – False or C – Can't say.

1. William's first construction on the site was built relatively quickly
2. The Crown Jewels are kept close to the river Thames
3. There was already a building on the site before 1070
4. The White Tower has not changed much since 1078
5. The White Tower is the largest structure on the site

Example F

'The genetic health of many breeds of dog has come under the spotlight recently; critics point to inbred defects that have a serious impact on the health and well-being of a significant number of pedigree animals. Defects such as hip dysplasia, breathing problems and syringomyelia (a particular problem in King Charles Spaniels) are held to be the result of breeding programmes that are aimed at producing aesthetically "perfect" dogs in terms of the breed standard rather than healthy animals. The BBC and the RSPCA have recently decided to withdraw support for Crufts, the premier dog show, in response to widespread disquiet that the Kennel Club and the dog breeding fraternity have done too little to tackle the issue.'

For each statement answer A – True; B – False or C – Can't say.

1. Non-pedigree dogs do not suffer from genetic defects
2. The RSPCA still support Crufts despite criticisms about dog health
3. Defects caused by breeding programmes include hip dysplasia and breathing problems
4. Some dog breeders have focused on the breed standard at the expense of animal health
5. The Kennel Club and Crufts are working to remedy the problem of inbreeding

Logic and logical relationships
(moderate/hard)

Example G

'The process of developing new drugs and new therapies is long and expensive. Pharmaceutical companies must overcome many obstacles before they can market a new drug. First they have to discover a new molecule which is not already the intellectual property of another company; they then have to prove that it is effective and safe. Many years are needed to complete all the trials required before a drug can be taken to market and most compounds – even promising ones – don't make it to the prescription list. The hit rate is low and people can spend their whole careers in pharmaceutical research and development without ever taking a drug all the way through this process. So expensive is drug development that big pharmaceutical companies need to be confident that the drug will have a large market when it has completed all the testing stages. For this reason, important areas of therapy can be neglected because too few people suffer from the illness to make it worth the investment. Large companies have to answer to their shareholders and, cynically, it can be argued that from a drug company point of view, the ideal drug is one that moderates symptoms – and thus has to be taken over a long period of time – rather than one which cures the disease and never needs to be taken again.'

For each statement answer A – True; B – False or C – Can't say.

1. Market factors will influence which drugs companies are willing to invest in
2. It cannot be said that drug companies need to be confident of a large market for their products
3. Most drugs have side effects so they have to be rigorously tested
4. The prescription list is made up of only a small proportion of the drugs that go through trials and testing
5. Discovering a new molecule is not the first stage in developing a new drug

Example H

'The Fender Stratocaster is probably the most widely used electric guitar in the world. It has been in continuous production since it was first designed by Leo Fender and his colleagues in 1954. It differs from earlier designs – such as the Telecaster – in a number of important ways, including the more comfortable contoured shape of the body and in terms of its electrical components. The Stratocaster has three single coil pick-ups in contrast to the Telecaster's two, and while the Telecaster can claim to be the solid-bodied guitar that has been in continuous production for longer, the 'Strat' – as the Stratocaster is usually known – has eclipsed it in terms of sales and fame. Strats are only built in the USA, Mexico, Japan and Korea, while a cheaper version – known as the Squier Strat – is also built under licence in China, Indonesia and India. The Stratocaster is known for its very clean, bright sound and the flexibility of tone provided by its three-way selector switch, which allows the player to decide which of the three pick-ups is being used to amplify the signal. Guitarists also discovered that by putting the switch in an intermediate position between pick-ups, a unique growling sound could be produced.'

For each statement answer A – True; B – False or C – Can't say.

1. It is not true to say that the Telecaster and the Stratocaster are broadly similar in design
2. The guitar that has been in production for longer also has three pick-ups
3. The contoured body and the number of pick-ups are only two of the ways in which the Strat and the Telecaster differ
4. Comfort is one of the factors that has led to increased sales of Stratocasters as compared to Telecasters
5. The Stratocaster gives guitarists more scope for experimentation and modification of the guitar

Example I

'The invention of the steam engine is most commonly associated with the names of Thomas Newcomen and James Watt, though in fact it was James Savery who first patented a crude steam engine in 1698. The industrial revolution and its demand for mineral resources meant that coal mining was a crucial enterprise and one of its most significant challenges was that of pumping water out of deep mines: it was this problem that Savery's steam engine solved. While Newcomen later improved this pump design and while the more charismatic applications of steam were to be credited to people such as James Watt and George Stephenson, the initial groundbreaking work was Savery's. Watt's key contribution – in his patent of 1769 – was the addition of a separate condenser that made steam engines much more efficient: this became the predominant design which served as the powerhouse for the industrial revolution. The expiry of this patent in 1800 opened the doors to inventors such as Trevithic and Stephenson who, with their patents for high-pressure engines, were then able to lay the foundations for the age of steam locomotion.'

For each statement answer A – True; B – False or C – Can't say.

1. People who built on the work of James Savery became more famous than Savery himself
2. Watt's patent was intermediate between those of Savery and Stephenson
3. Trevithic and Stephenson had been working on their steam engine designs prior to 1800
4. Savery's steam engine design was too weak to be used in deep mines
5. It would not be true to say that Watt's contribution made steam engines slightly more effective
6. Watt and Stephenson were more charismatic than Savery and Newcomen
7. A number of people deserve credit for developing the steam engine, no one person made a pioneering contribution

Word meaning/vocabulary

The format of word meaning or vocabulary tests you will most commonly encounter is, again, based on reading a short passage but this time being asked questions about specific words in the passage. As usual you will be given a multiple response choice from which to select your answer. An easy and a hard example are given below.

Example J (easy)

*'Few people can afford to be **complacent** about their pensions in the current situation, particularly those of us depending on private pensions. The poor performance of the stock market over the last 10 years means that pension funds have not delivered their promised rates of return and for a lot of us this means substantially less income to see us through retirement. Most **independent** pensions advisers are saying that private pensions are underinvested by about 40%, meaning that the **average** saver needs to be investing £5,000 more each year than they currently do if they want to protect their retirement income. Whether you are planning to buy an annuity or whether you have other plans for investing your pension pot on retirement, chances are that it will not deliver what you expect.'*

1. **Which of these words would best replace the word *complacent* in the first sentence?**

   a. Easy
   b. Satisfied
   c. Compliant
   d. Anxious
   e. Conducive

2. **Which of these words would best replace the word *average* in the third sentence?**

   a. Mean
   b. Typical
   c. Normal
   d. Irregular
   e. Concerned

3. **Which of these words means the opposite of *independent*?**

   a. Reliant

   b. Qualified

   c. Self-sufficient

   d. Objective

   e. Isolated

Example K (hard)

*'Arguments in health economics are always challenging ones; the fundamental difficulty of **aligning** scarce resources with apparently infinite demand means that prioritising – in itself problematic and subject to multiple sources of influence – becomes as much a political as a scientific or strictly **rational** process. Health economists find relatively little difficulty in calculating return on investment for a particular **therapeutic** intervention (for example in terms of speed of recovery), or in estimating average individual benefit in terms of quality of life or extended life expectancy, but find it much more difficult to provide an "economic" answer as to the value of newer therapeutic options such as fertility treatment where the payoff is hard to define in individual or societal terms but is, rather, a matter of personal well-being or even human rights. As a result, the economic arguments for supporting or **proscribing** a therapy will never be the only consideration when it comes to making difficult decisions about how to ration health care.'*

1. **Which of these words is closest in meaning to the word 'aligning' in the first sentence?**

   a. Comparing

   b. Agreeing

   c. Convincing

   d. Matching

   e. Accepting

2. **Which of these words would best replace the word 'rational' in the first sentence?**

   a. Cognitive
   b. Objective
   c. Decisive
   d. Numerical
   e. Reasonable

3. **Which of these words means the opposite of 'therapeutic' in the second sentence?**

   a. Injurious
   b. Restorative
   c. Remedial
   d. Alternative
   e. Harmless

4. **Which of these words means the same as 'proscribing' in the final sentence?**

   a. Permitting
   b. Legalising
   c. Undermining
   d. Prohibiting
   e. Preventing

Remember that some tests combine all these formats; in other words, a passage is followed by questions about comprehension, logic and word meanings. The principles are exactly the same as above, however, and familiarity with these items should help to remove a lot of the anxiety about this kind of test.

Verbal Tests – Answers

Example A

The answers are   1 – b   2 – d   3 – c

The answers are simply based on an accurate reading of the passage; the only point to watch out for here is to make sure you base your answer to Q3 purely on the passage and not on your own views – for example regarding whether science used to be taught better!

Example B

The answers are   1 – e   2 – a   3 – b

Again, accurate reading of the passage and careful reading of the question is what is needed here. For Q1, only choice (e) is factually correct based on the information in the passage; some of the other statements might be possible explanations but not from the facts given. For Q2, choice (a) has the same meaning as the first sentence in the passage because it is the only statement that points out that complacency is a particular problem for people with private pensions. For Q3, answer (b) is the fullest summary; the other options make reference to only a small part of the passage, or are offering an opinion rather than a summary.

Example C

The answers are   1 – c   2 – b   3 – b   4 – b

Careful reading of the question becomes still more important as the items become more complex. Often, the difficulty level comes from having to choose a 'best fit' answer rather than one that is absolutely correct. One of the alternatives they give you will be better than the others, however, and this is what you must look out for. For example, in Q1 above, none of the pairs provides a complete answer to the question 'what are the reasons for a lack of creativity', but this is not what they are asking! They are asking for which pair *best* describes reasons for a lack of creativity – in other words which pair comes closest to explaining – and (c) is the only answer that contains two inhibitors of creativity.

Example D

The answers are: 1 – b   2 – b   3 – c   4 – a

The principles here are the same as for the other passages – namely, the need for careful reading and the need to base your answers only on the information provided. The challenge here is that the passage is more complex, with more sub-clauses and trickier language. If we unpick the specific questions:

■ Q1 – all of the potential answers are plausible conclusions that you could draw from the information given, but only (b) is an *explanation* of why health care decisions are difficult and this is what the question asks for.

■ Q2 – answer (a) is a close replacement for the final sentence but answer (b) is better because it makes specific reference to one of the factors – namely economics – which is a closer paraphrasing of the final sentence. Answer (c) is a broad conclusion not a paraphrasing of the last sentence and answer (d) does not make any of the same points as are covered in the last sentence.

■ Q3 – the first three option answers are all conclusions you could reasonably draw from the passage but only answer (c) summarises the gist of what has been said. Answer (d) is a statement of opinion and not a summary.

■ Q4 – only answer (a) is factually accurate; the others are plausible – even common sense – opinions but you can't defend them purely based on the information given.

Example E

The answers are: 1 – A   2 – A   3 – C   4 – B   5 – C

Hopefully you won't have had too much trouble with these questions, but just to help you check the logic:

Q1 True: the passage clearly states this.

Q2 True: the passage tells you that the Crown Jewels are in the Tower and that the Tower is close to the Thames, it follows logically that the jewels are kept close to the Thames.

Q3 Can't say: there is no information in the passage about any earlier building; now, you might happen to know that there was a Roman fort on the site 1,000 years earlier, but *you can't deduce this from the information in the passage*!

Q4 False: the passage clearly states that the White Tower has been added to and improved; therefore it is incorrect to say that it has not changed much.

Q5 Can't say: again, the passage gives you no information about this.

Example F
The answers are: 1 – C   2 – B   3 – A   4 – A   5 – C

Here is a quick walk through the logic of these answers:

Q1 Can't say: the passage makes no mention of problems with non-pedigree dogs; it might be implied that pedigree animals have more problems, but from the passage alone, you can't say. Watch out too for double negatives in this kind of question – non-pedigree ... do not suffer – they are sometimes used to make interpretation more difficult.

Q2 False: the passage is clear that the RSPCA has withdrawn support.

Q3 True: factually true based on the information given.

Q4 True: this is a clear logical conclusion you can draw from the information given.

Q5 Can't say: while it might be likely that these organisations are working on the problem, you do not have any evidence of it from the passage.

Example G
The answers are: 1 – A   2 – B   3 – C   4 – A   5 – B
Once again, the logic is as follows:

Q1 True: the passage states that companies need to be confident of a large market so it follows that this will influence which drugs they invest in.

Q2 False: it *can* be said that drug companies need a large market, so this statement is false.

Q3 Can't say: you might think this from your own knowledge but you are not explicitly told it in the passage.

Q4 True: you are told that most drugs don't make it to the prescription list so it follows logically that only a small proportion of the drugs tested do make it through to the list.

Q5 False: you are told that discovering a new molecule *is* the first stage; this statement contradicts that so it must be false.

Example H

The answers are: 1 – A   2 – B   3 – A   4 – A   5 – C
Here is a quick run through the logic:

Q1 True: here is another of those double negatives – it is true to say that it is not true to say – the passage tells you that there are important differences in design, so a statement saying that 'it is not true to say that they are broadly similar' has to be true.

Q2 False: the guitar that has been in production for longer is the Telecaster and the passage tells you that the Telecaster has only two pick-ups.

Q3 True: the passage tells you that 'there are a number of ways' in which they differ of which contour and number of pick-ups are only two, therefore the statement is true.

Q4 True: the passage tells you that the Stratocaster has 'eclipsed' sales of the Telecaster (meaning it sells a lot more) and that the comfortable contoured shape is one of the improvements over the Telecaster; it therefore follows logically that comfort *is* one of the factors leading to increased sales.

Q5 Can't say: the passage does not give you enough information to draw this conclusion; while the passage does state that guitarists have discovered novel ways of using the controls on the Stratocaster, it says nothing about how much it is possible to experiment with the Telecaster.

Example I

The answers are: 1 – A   2 – A   3 – C   4 – B   5 – A   6 – C
7 – B

Once again, here is the logic:

Q1 True: it is a reasonable inference from the information in the passage,
namely that developments in early steam engine design are more often
associated with names other than Savery's. You may need to be careful
with this question because it is an example of one where – for once – your
common sense and the requirements of the question might line up. In
other words, your common knowledge might tell you that Watt is more
famous than Savery (and could lead you to second-guess the question as
in earlier examples) but in fact this conclusion is *also* a logical conclusion
from the information you are given!

Q2 True: careful reading is all that is required here; Watt's patent came after
Savery's and before Stephenson's.

Q3 Can't say: the information in the passage does not tell you what Trevithic
and Stephenson were up to before 1800.

Q4 False: the passage clearly states that the problem of pumping water out of
deep mines was what Savery's engine solved.

Q5 True: this is another of those double negatives; Watt's design made steam
engines considerably more effective (not slightly more), so it is true to say
that a statement claiming this to be false is indeed correct (or true!).

Q6 Can't say: the passage does not give you any information about this, it
mentions *more charismatic applications* but does not comment on the
charisma of the individuals.

Q7 False: the passage clearly states that 'the groundbreaking work was
Savery's', telling us that he did indeed make a pioneering contribution, so
the statement is false.

Example J

The answers are: 1 – b   2 – b   3 – a

Hopefully, not too much of a problem with these: as usual you need to read the question carefully. In the first two questions you are asked for the best replacement word – meaning that you have to take the context into account. In other words, which of the alternatives would work best *in this sentence*? You can sometimes be asked to identify a word of similar or opposite meaning without reference to the context, so watch out for these.

Example K

The answers are: 1 – d   2 – b   3 – d   4 – a

The harder questions of this type usually depend on more obscure words or on more subtle differences in meaning, for example, the difference between 'prohibiting' and 'preventing' in question 3. (To be pedantic – prevent is a more causative verb implying direct intervention to stop something from happening; prohibit implies a rule or law to more indirectly stop something from happening – this is the meaning that is closest to the context of the example.) Once again, careful reading of the question is important.

IN A NUTSHELL

There are a number of reasons why you might get a score lower than you deserve when completing verbal reasoning tests, for example: lack of familiarity with the test format, nervousness and poor preparation. Avoid these pitfalls by:

■ Practising – make sure you understand the logic of the examples contained in this chapter.

■ Developing your test taking skills as you work through the examples. Recognise when you tend to get stuck and you are better served by moving on to the next item.

■ Reading questions very carefully to make sure you understand what is being asked of you, you can waste a lot of time otherwise.

■ Developing your own sense of which kinds of item you find easy or hard – use this to focus your practice.

Above all – don't panic!

4 ABSTRACT REASONING TESTS

This chapter aims to familiarise you with the different types of abstract reasoning tests. You will also get a chance to practise them extensively. You will understand:

■ The different types of 'rules' that are used in abstract reasoning questions

■ How to do your best by focusing on one aspect of the question at a time

■ How to use the multiple-choice options to help identify the correct answer

■ Which types of questions you are best at and where you need to gain more practice

What abstract reasoning tests measure

Of all the psychometric tests you might complete, abstract reasoning tests will 'look' the most unusual and unconventional, that is the questions do not look like typical business problems. Instead, you will be given diagrams consisting of shapes, signs or symbols, as you will see from the practice questions in this chapter. So why are these tests used? Despite their strange appearance, the questions in abstract reasoning tests measure important qualities. Employers use these tests when they want to understand how well you can:

- Identify patterns or 'rules' in complex data
- Separate what is important from what is irrelevant
- Deal with and interpret complexity
- Apply insights to solve problems

In abstract reasoning tests, each question works by following a particular rule or set of rules

How abstract reasoning tests work

Although there are many different formats, abstract reasoning tests involve one of two general methods:

- **Series** – identifying the next pattern in a series of patterns.
- **Categories** – identifying which pattern 'belongs' to a group of patterns.

Whichever method tests use, each question works by following a particular rule or set of rules. To answer the questions successfully you will need to identify which rule or rules are being used.

Let's look at an example of a series-based question:

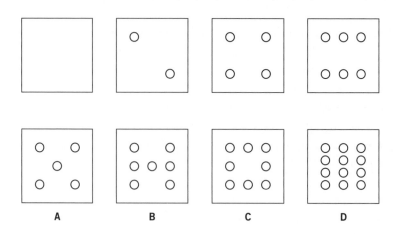

Here there is only one rule operating and that rule quickly becomes apparent. We can see that two circles are added each time, so the correct answer is option C – the next pattern in the sequence is 8 circles.

Let's look at an example of a category-based question.

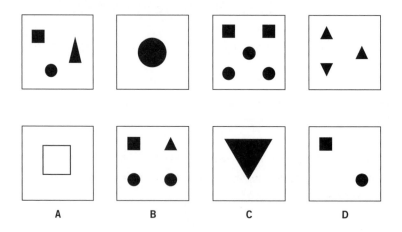

Here there are two rules in operation. The first, and most obvious, is that all of the shapes are black. The second is that there are an odd number of shpaes in each pattern. So the correct answer is option C. The questions become harder if the rule is more difficult to spot or if more than one rule is applied at the same time. What might make a rule more difficult to spot? Rules can be based on any aspect of the shapes within a pattern. Table 4.1 shows just some of the ways in which rules can be applied.

Table 4.1

Rule	Examples
Shape	The shape remains consistent, e.g. all triangles
	The shapes change in a cyclical pattern, e.g. square, then circle, then triangle, then back to square
	The shapes share common features, e.g. all are curved, straight-lined, or enclosed
Colour	Colour remains constant
	Colours change in a cyclical pattern
	Colours combine to form a new colour
Size	Size remains constant
	Size changes in a progressive pattern (e.g. small, medium, large)
Number	Each pattern has a constant number of shapes
	The number of shapes changes in a progressive or cyclical pattern
Rotation	Patterns revolve clockwise or anti-clockwise
	Patterns are inverted
Lines of symmetry	Patterns are symmetrical or non-symmetrical
	Patterns share the same lines of symmetry
	Lines of symmetry rotate
Merging	Two shapes overlap to form a new pattern
	Two shapes overlap and cancel each other out (e.g. two squares overlap exactly and disappear)

Remember, Table 4.1 shows just some of the rules that are used in abstract reasoning questions. In practice, you are likely to come across these and other rules. So what is the best way to tackle these types of questions?

Tips for top scores

Focus on one rule at a time

As you will see from the practice questions in this chapter, harder questions tend to have more complicated patterns where there is lots of information to take in. When faced with questions like these, it is all too easy to panic and stare at the shapes without taking anything in.

The most important tactic is to work systematically – like a detective – through one possibility at a time. Focus on one hypothesis and investigate until you have proved or discounted it. This disciplined, systematic approach will allow you to work through the questions as quickly and clearly as possible. It saves the confusion and wasted effort of half-exploring a possibility, moving on to others, and then having to revisit it again.

Work systematically through one possibility at a time

Use the 'answer patterns' to help

Whichever format an abstract reasoning test uses, each question will have two components:

■ Question patterns – which present the problem that needs to be solved
■ Answer patterns – which are the multiple choice answers that can be given

Some answer patterns will be related to the question patterns and others won't. The most obvious approach is to examine the question patterns and try to determine the link between them, which will then show which of the answer patterns are correct. A better approach, however, is to make full use of all the data you have available – the question patterns and the answer patterns. Knowing that some of the answer patterns will be right and some of them will be wrong means that you can look for differences between them.

A good starting point is to check if any of the answer patterns are obviously different from the other answer and question patterns. If you can spot the difference, it's often easy to identify the rule or rules at play. For example, one of the answer patterns may miss an element that is included in most of the other patterns, such as a black triangle, or a line of symmetry. Remember when using this technique that the 'odd' answer patterns may be different because they exclude or include elements.

PRACTICE QUESTIONS

(answers can be found at the end of the chapter on page 104)

In the rest of this chapter we give you a number of examples of abstract reasoning questions to try out, together with correct answers and the logic used to solve the question. We have rated the questions as easy, moderate and hard. This will help you to get a sense of which questions or question formats you find easiest or most difficult and to plan your practice accordingly.

In turn, the practice examples will cover:

- Series-based formats
- Category-based formats

Series

In each of these practice questions there are eight patterns. The four patterns that run along the top are the 'question patterns'. The four patterns in the row beneath are the multiple choice 'answer patterns' which are labelled A, B, C and D. To answer the question correctly you need to identify which one of the answer patterns in the bottom row continues the series in the top row.

Series (easy)

1.

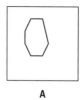

| A | B | C | D |

2.

  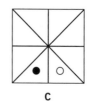 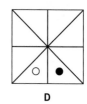

| A | B | C | D |

3.

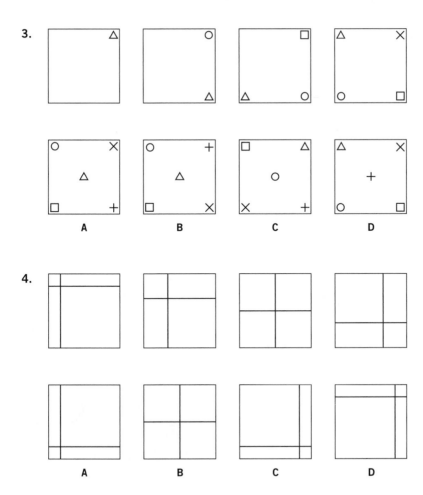

4.

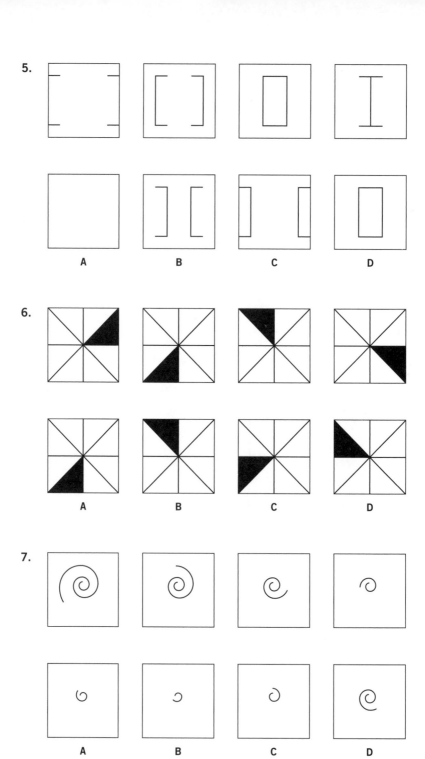

5.

6.

7.

Series (moderate)

8.

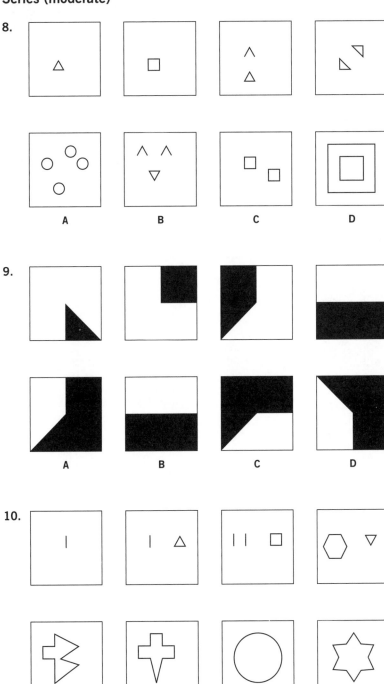

11.

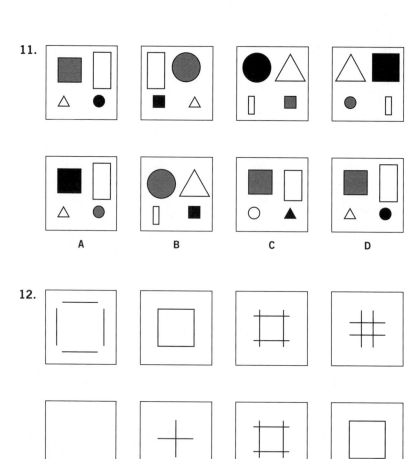

12.

13.

   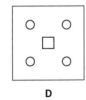

    A   B   C   D

14.

 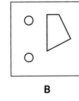  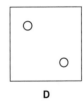

    A   B   C   D

Series (hard)

15.

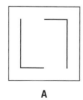

A   B   C   D

16.

A   B   C   D

17.

A	B	C	D

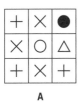 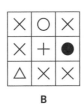 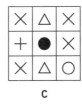 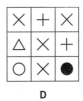

A	B	C	D

18.

△	+	+
×	△	○
●	+	●

+	●	×
△	○	+
×	●	△

○	●	+
●	+	×
×	×	△

×	×	+
○	△	×
+	●	×

+	×	●
×	○	△
+	×	+

×	○	×
×	+	●
△	×	×

×	△	×
+	●	×
×	△	○

×	+	×
△	×	+
○	×	●

A	B	C	D

19.

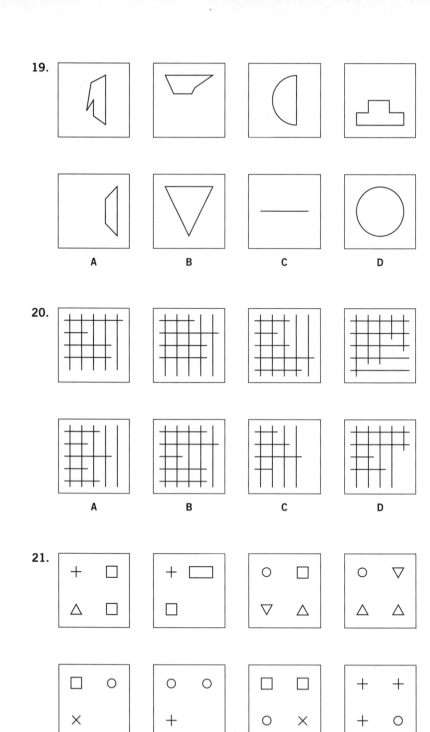

20.

21.

Categories

The four patterns that run along the top are the 'question patterns'. The four patterns in the row beneath are the multiple choice 'answer patterns', which are labelled A, B, C and D. The question patterns always have at least one characteristic in common. To answer each question correctly, you need to identify which two of the answer patterns shares that same characteristic.

Categories (easy)

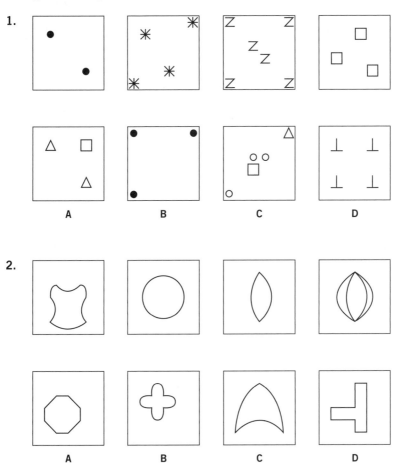

3.

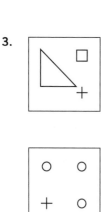 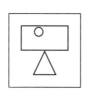

 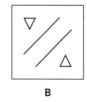 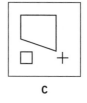 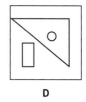

A   B   C   D

4.

 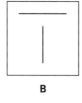 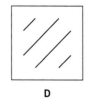

A   B   C   D

5.

   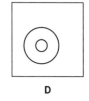

A   B   C   D

6.

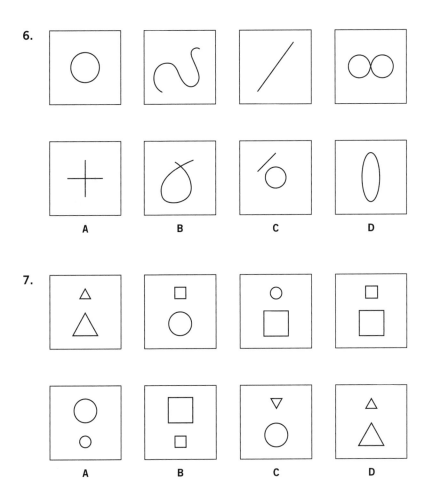

7.

Categories (moderate)

8.

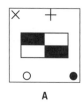

A   B   C   D

9.

   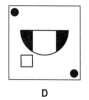

A   B   C   D

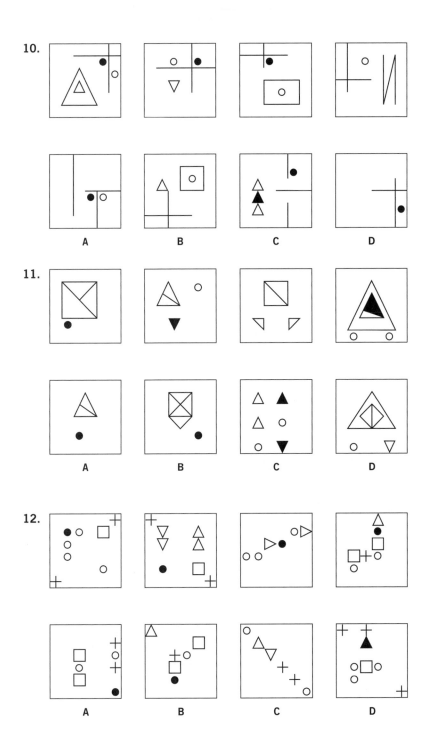

10.

11.

12.

13.

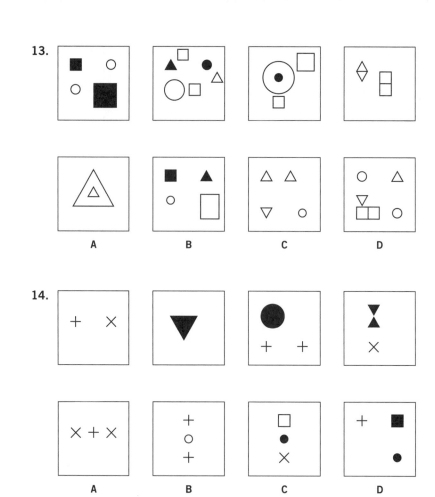

14.

Categories (hard)

15.

| A | B | C | D |

16.

   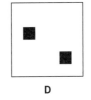

| A | B | C | D |

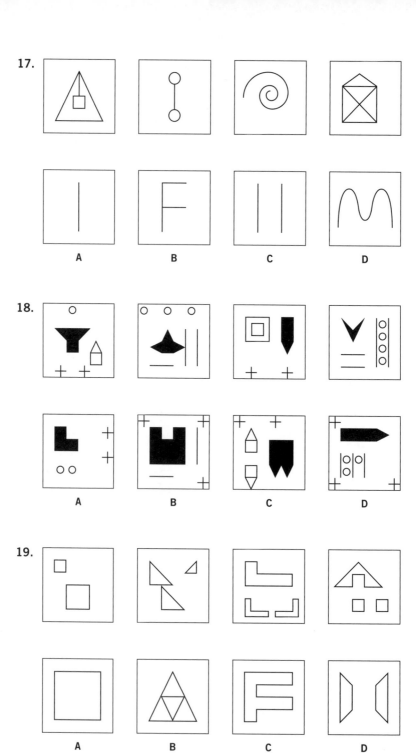

17.

A   B   C   D

18.

A   B   C   D

19.

A   B   C   D

20.

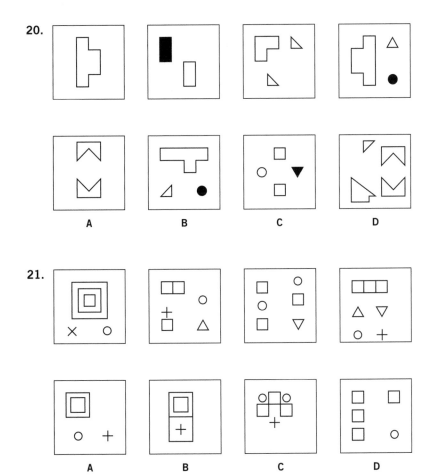

21.

Abstract Reasoning Tests – Answers

Answers – Series questions (easy)

Q1 Each shape has one more side than the previous shape, so option A is correct.

Q2 The white circle moves one space anti-clockwise and the black moves one space clockwise, so option C is correct.

Q3 The objects follow the triangle, so option B is correct.

Q4 The vertical line moves right and the horizontal line moves down, so option C is correct.

Q5 The shapes move in opposite directions, so option B is correct.

Q6 The dark segment moves three spaces clockwise each time, so option C is correct.

Q7 The spiral gets shorter each time, so option C is correct.

Answers – Series questions (moderate)

Q8 Each pattern has an extra line each time, so option B is correct as it has seven lines.

Q9 The black area grows by one-eighth and the pattern rotates 90 degrees anti-clockwise, so option D is correct.

Q10 The shape on the left of each pattern has the same number of lines as all of the shapes in the previous pattern combined. So option A is correct as it has nine lines.

Q11 The shapes rotate anti-clockwise, the patterns rotate clockwise, and the shapes on the top are always larger, so option D is correct.

Q12 The four lines gradually converge, so option B is correct.

Q13 The circle gets bigger each time, so option B is correct.

Q14 The number of symmetrical shapes increases by one each time, so option A is correct.

Answers – Series questions (hard)

Q15 Each pattern has one more line than the previous pattern, so option C is correct as it comprises 10 lines.

Q16 The line of symmetry in each pattern alternates between horizontal and vertical, so option A is correct as it has a horizontal line of symmetry.

Q17 The line of symmetry rotates 45 degrees clockwise, starting with a vertical line of symmetry for the first pattern, so option C is correct as it has a vertical (180 degrees) line of symmetry.

Q18 An extra 'X' is added each time, so option B is correct.

Q19 The longest line of each shape rotates 90 degrees anti-clockwise, so option A is correct.

Q20 The number of times that two lines cross increases by one each time, so option B is correct.

Q21 The number of horizontal lines decreases by one each time, so option A is correct.

Answers – Categories questions (easy)

Q1 Each pattern is made up of identical shapes, so options B and D are correct.

Q2 Each pattern is made up of curved lines, so options B and C are correct.

Q3 Each pattern contains a triangle, so options B and D are correct.

Q4 The lines in each pattern are always parallel, so options C and D are correct.

Q5 The shapes in each pattern get bigger, so options B and D are correct.

Q6 Each shape contains only one line, so options B and D are correct.

Q7 In each pattern the largest shape is at the bottom, so options C and D are correct.

Answers – Categories questions (moderate)

Q8 Each pattern has a shape which is 'open', so options A and D are correct.

Q9 Each pattern has a shape or symbol in one corner with another shape or symbol diagonally opposite, so options A and D are correct. Notice how many other shapes there are to distract your attention.

Q10 Each pattern contains lines that cross, so options B and D are correct.

Q11 Each pattern contains four triangles, so options C and D are correct.

Q12 Each pattern contains a black circle, so options A and B are correct.

Q13 In each pattern there is two of every shape, so options A and D are correct.

Q14 None of the shapes are 'hollow', so options A and D are correct.

Answers – Categories questions (hard)

Q15 The shapes in each pattern only occupy one half of the box, so options A and C are correct.

Q16 Each pattern contains a vowel, so options B and D are correct. Note that most abstract reasoning questions are designed so that they can be solved without any prior knowledge (e.g. about vowels and consonants), although this is not always the case.

Q17 Each pattern can be drawn without going over the same line twice, or taking the pencil off the paper, so options A and D are correct.

Q18 All of the black shapes in each pattern have a vertical line of symmetry, so options B and C are correct.

Q19 All of the patterns contain at least one right angle, so options A and C are correct.

Q20 Each pattern contains eight right-angles, so options C and D are correct.

Q21 Each pattern contains three squares, so options B and C are correct.

IN A NUTSHELL

In abstract reasoning tests, each question works by following a particular rule or set of rules.

- The key to answering abstract reasoning questions correctly is identifying the 'rules' that are being used.
- Remember that the rules can go from the tangible (e.g. the number of shapes) through to the very abstract (e.g. patterns that can only be drawn by taking your pencil off the paper, or going over the same line twice!).
- Use the 'answer patterns' as well as the 'question patterns' to identify the rules by spotting the odd one out.
- Don't become overwhelmed by complex patterns – focus on just one hypothesis at a time.

5 KNOWLEDGE AND SKILLS TESTS

In this chapter you will be introduced to knowledge and skills tests that are sometimes used by employers. You will understand:

- The differences between knowledge and skills tests

- The most common types of knowledge and skills tests

- How to perform at your best in these tests

What are tests of knowledge and skills?

The three most common types of ability tests are numerical, verbal and abstract reasoning, which are covered in Chapters 2, 3 and 4. Although they are much less common, you might come across other types of psychometric tests designed to measure specific knowledge and skills. Remember to always ask the recruiter what kind of test you will be taking!

Tests of knowledge

Tests of knowledge measure how much information, or expertise, a candidate has about a specific business area.

Tests of knowledge include:

- Mechanical comprehension
- Book-keeping and payroll
- Linguistics (e.g. ability to speak and understand a foreign language such as German or Mandarin)
- Computer programming and website design

A knowledge test will include multiple-choice or 'yes/no' questions about specific aspects of a business area. An example is given below.

International Financial Reporting Standards (IFRS) financial statements consist of which of the following?

Item	Yes	No
A Statement of Financial Position		
A comprehensive income statement		
Either a statement of changes in equity (SOCE) or a statement of recognised income or expense (SORIE)		
Receipts for expenses		
The home address of the chief finance officer		
A cashflow statement or statement of cashflows		
Notes, including a summary of the significant accounting policies		

Unlike other psychometric tests, knowledge tests are very specific in that they focus on a specialist area of knowledge or expertise. As a result, the answers cannot easily be guessed. However, unlike other tests we have described, the information that these tests deal with is learnable, given sufficient time.

Tests of skill

Tests of skill measure how well a candidate can execute a certain task. Skills that employers may wish to test include:

- **Emotional intelligence** – the ability to identify and understand emotions.
- **Spatial awareness** – the ability to understand the relative position and rotation of objects.
- **Touch-typing** – the ability to type quickly and accurately use the touch-typing technique.

For example, given three pages of handwritten notes, or a 20-minute recording of a meeting, how quickly and accurately can a candidate type this information? An emotional intelligence test presents pictures and written scenarios and requires candidates to identify the emotions (or the most appropriate emotions) given the picture shown or the situation described. See the example below.

Simon is about to meet his new line manager for the first time. As he knocks to enter the office, Simon can hear him shouting angrily down the telephone. To what extent will Simon feel the following?

	Not at all		Moderately		Very strongly
	1	2	3	4	5
Anxious					
Angry					
Self-conscious					
Relieved					

This question is about understanding emotions – recognising which emotions are most likely to occur in different situations. In this question we would expect Simon to feel anxious and, as a result, somewhat self-conscious, although he is unlikely to feel relieved or angry. Let's look at another example.

Alice is about to give a presentation at a conference where many of the delegates are potential customers. How helpful will the following emotions be?

	Not helpful at all		Somewhat helpful		Very helpful
	1	2	3	4	5
Apprehension					
Acceptance					
Joy					
Vigilance					
Surprise					
Boredom					
Serenity					

In this question, we can expect positive emotions such as joy to be helpful, along with some degree of nervousness which will provide the necessary urgency and adrenaline! Less helpful will be emotions that can serve to inhibit or distract, such as surprise and boredom. To see other examples of emotional intelligence questions, visit the Emotional Intelligence & MSCEIT 2, 3, 4 website (www.emotionaliq.org/MSCEITExamples.htm).

Remember to always ask the recruiter what kind of test you will be taking.

Unlike the tests described in chapters 2, 3 and 4, which are used by recruiters for a wide variety of roles and industries, knowledge and skill tests tend to be used in more specific circumstances and within specific industries. For example, we worked with a telecoms business to develop a skills test for recruiting call centre staff. The test simulated the computer systems that the staff used when taking customer calls. The company wanted to select candidates who were able to use Information Technology effectively to provide excellent customer service. Candidates who took the test were shown how to use the simulated computer system. They then received calls from assessors, who were acting as customers. Using the test the company was able to assess how well candidates navigated the computer system to find the relevant information, and how accurately and quickly they relayed it.

Tips for top scores

Practice

Like all skills, we can improve our abilities – and therefore our scores in the knowledge and skills types of test – through practice. If you are considering a career which has specific skill requirements, think about activities that you can practice, which will develop your skills. This could involve at-work tasks or social activities such as volunteering or sports.

Make full use of free resources

Aside from paid-for professional training courses, there are several excellent – and free – sources of information if you need to improve your knowledge in a specific area. The following lists gives just some examples:

- iTunes U (www.apple.com/support/itunes_u/) – this service is provided as part of Apple's iTunes software and is free to download from the Apple website. From iTunes you can access sound recordings and accompanying course notes from a wide range of educational lectures and topics. These resources are provided by many leading universities including Harvard, Yale, Stanford, Oxford and Cambridge.
- Open Yale Courses (http://oyc.yale.edu) – this website is hosted by Yale University and includes course materials and videos of lectures on a range of introductory courses.
- Google Scholar beta (http://scholar.google.co.uk) – the Google scholar website searches many journals and peer-reviewed articles based on the key words you enter. Although some of the content is restricted access, for example because it is sold by publishers, look for PDF format articles that are downloadable for free. Let's say you want to learn about the Prince2 project management methodology. Typing 'Prince2' into Google Scholar

returns a few books and citations, but the fifth link (at the time of writing) is a free-access PDF document titled 'Understanding Prince2'. At 247 pages, it should be enough to give you a thorough introduction!

IN A NUTSHELL

For certain jobs that require specific knowledge and skills, potential employers can ask you to take a test that examines your existing knowledge and skills in that area. Remember that:

- Tests of knowledge ask very specific questions about an area of expertise, such as financial reporting, web design or project management methodology.
- Tests of skill measure how well something can be done, such as recognising emotions or touch-typing.
- Knowledge and skills can be improved through practice – take advantage of freely available online resources, work-based projects and social activities.

6 PERSONALITY AND PREFERENCE TESTS

As well as measures of specific ability such as numerical and verbal reasoning, it is now common for organisations to include measures of personality as part of their selection processes. So what are they trying to discover about you by using such tests? In this chapter we will:

- Explain what these tests are trying to measure and how these tests are used by organisations

- Give you the chance to rate yourself on some of the main personality dimensions

- Help you to build your self-awareness

- Explain different response formats and the main tests you can expect to encounter

What personality and preference tests measure

As mentioned in Chapter 1, personality and preference tests are based on the idea that there are elements of our character, personality, habits or work style that are relatively stable across our life, and that these have some bearing on how effectively we will perform in a job. So, for example, personality tests try to explore qualities such as:

- How well are you likely to work as part of a team?
- Do you have a strong preference for independence and autonomy or do you prefer to work collaboratively?
- Are you extraverted and talkative or do you prefer quiet time in which to reflect?
- Are you the big-picture thinker who gets frustrated by detail or are you structured and a perfectionist?
- Are you an analytical problem-solver who likes data or are you a creative and imaginative problem-solver?
- Do you prefer to work in a focused way, concentrating on one thing at a time, or do you value flexibility and the chance to multi-task?

These are the kinds of 'preferences' that personality tests are trying to get at.

There are important differences between personality tests and ability tests. Perhaps the most important difference is that preference tests do not have an objectively 'right' answer; however, employers would not be using them if they did not think that they provided information that helps them to differentiate between people who are more or less suited to a particular role. This said, in general you should not worry about answering questions in the way that you think they want – there are dangers in doing this. It also means that for personality tests there is only one top tip, namely – BE YOURSELF!

ASSESSING PERSONALITY

When employers are recruiting, they are often just as worried about making a mistake and getting the wrong person – someone who just won't fit in – as they are about selecting the best person for the job. When we talk to employers, they usually have a broad idea about the kinds of personal characteristics that they think a given job requires, but they also have a view about the kind of person who is unlikely to do well. For example, in a recent project we worked with a large retailer to identify the key attributes needed by its managers. Just as important as any specific experience or knowledge was their approach to customer service and their approach to working with their colleagues. While they wanted people who were commercially competitive, they certainly did not want people who would be selfish at the expense of their team mates or at the expense of customer service. They felt that getting this wrong would be a bigger risk than any particular knowledge that a new manager might be missing. For this employer, assessing a potential recruit's personality, style or preferences is a way of helping to manage this risk.

Personality tests are based on your self-report; in other words, the interpretation of your 'style' that they give can only be as accurate as your responses to the questions. (There is no evidence for so-called 'objective' measures of personality, such as interpretation of handwriting or ink blots. You should be suspicious of any organisation that uses them.)

Being yourself

For some of us this is easier said than done. The reason is that some of us are just more self-aware than others and find it easier to answer questions about how we would respond 'on average' or about our 'typical' preferences or ways of responding to certain situations.

Take a question like the following one – it is quite typical of the kind of question you find in personality tests:

'In social situations I usually prefer to wait for others to approach me rather than actively joining the conversation'

Here comes the usual multiple-choice response format:

1. Strongly agree
2. Agree
3. Neither agree nor disagree
4. Disagree
5. Strongly disagree

Now, suppose you answer 'strongly disagree': in other words you feel you **are** the kind of person who quickly goes up to other people and starts chatting to them. But are you right? How much insight do you have to your behaviour in situations like this? Is it something you have thought about? What if sometimes you do, and sometimes you don't? What if it depends on the kind of social situation or the kind of people involved?

Good test designers go to a lot of trouble to create questions that people will be able to relate to and that they will find relatively easy to answer. However, they depend on your ability to answer such questions 'on average' or in terms of what you would typically do. This in turn depends on your ability to look at your own behaviour fairly objectively. So, how can you tell how self-aware you are?

One way is to ask yourself or your friends the questions overleaf; rate yourself – or get them to rate you – on a 10-point scale.

How open to new experiences am I – am I typically quite adventurous or more cautious in the kinds of situations I seek out?

Cautious   Adventurous

1   2   3   4   5   6   7   8   9   10

How conscientious am I – am I usually pretty organised, punctual and disciplined in the way I go about things or am I typically more free-wheeling in my approach?

Free-wheeling   Conscientious

1   2   3   4   5   6   7   8   9   10

How extraverted am I – am I usually a very sociable person, seeking out people and being chatty, or am I usually more reserved, quiet and needing time on my own?

Reserved   Extraverted

1   2   3   4   5   6   7   8   9   10

How agreeable am I – would people describe me as kind, thoughtful and considerate or am I seen as more objective, critical and 'tell it like it is'?

Critical   Agreeable

1   2   3   4   5   6   7   8   9   10

How anxious am I – am I the kind of person who is seldom stressed or nervous, or am I more emotional, showing my feelings and often working under a lot of pressure?

Calm   Anxious

1   2   3   4   5   6   7   8   9   10

If you and your friends' ratings are within a couple of points of each other, you probably have pretty good self-awareness. This means that when you fill out a personality test, the results will be in line with what you would expect. If there are significant differences between your ratings and your friends' ratings, this suggests that you might have some 'blind spots' in terms of your self-assessment. This exercise in itself will help you to re-evaluate and re-calibrate your perception of yourself.

How the test results are used

Unlike ability tests, personality tests are harder to use to predict work performance, for the simple reason that there is often more than one 'right way' to do a job well. Thus it isn't easy to say what kinds of personality characteristics will predict effective job performance. For example, suppose a recruiter is looking for sales representatives; you might think it would make sense for them to look for extraverted, sociable, talkative people who will have the 'gift of the gab' and will relate well to customers. This is fine in theory, but in reality, if that person is going to have to spend much of the working day alone in a car, driving from customer to customer, what is that going to do for their motivation and effectiveness?

Remember that an extravert is someone who needs people, who likes sociable working environments. A well-advised recruiter might recognise this and avoid people who are too extraverted. You, on the other hand, as an applicant, might be assuming that they will value extraverted tendencies and, as a result might try to enhance this aspect of your style as you fill out a personality test. This is why we say – BE YOURSELF. It seldom pays to second-guess the test or what an employer is looking for.

Personality tests are quite expensive for employers to use because the test publishers and the British Psychological Society insist that people should be trained to use and interpret them. So how – and – why do businesses use them?

Most business psychologists would not recommend that people be selected for jobs on the basis of personality tests alone. More typical uses for personality tests as part of selection are given below.

Screening

Some employers will use questionnaires about motivation and preferences as a way of sifting out people who they think will be unsuited to a particular task. They might, for example, disregard the applicants who are highly strategic and conceptual for a role which is operational, repetitive and administrative.

If you fill out such tests honestly you will be doing yourself a favour as you would be unlikely to enjoy or perform well in any kind of work which requires you to behave in ways that are completely contrary to your preferences.

Employers who use tests in this way are running the risk of recruiting 'clones' rather than people who can grow and develop in their business. However, be aware that they will usually be basing this practice on past experience of the kind of people who thrive or who flourish or wither in a particultar role.

Fitting in

Sometimes employers will be looking for an individual to fit in to a particular team or work group. At senior level this might be a specific search for someone strategic to balance the skills of a team that is very operational, or for someone very creative to enhance a team that is very practical. The personality test will never be the only source of information they are using but it will often be used to back up other data. (See the section 'Additional information to support other selection techniques' below.)

Worrying signs

For some roles, again usually at middle to senior level, the employer might be looking for signs of any extreme characteristics – sometimes called de-railing characteristics – such as extreme competitiveness or extreme non-compliance with rules and procedures. People with such 'dark side' characteristics often do quite well in organisations – up to a point. This is because it can make them very entrepreneurial and willing to take risks. However, at some point these extremes usually get them – and the organisation – into trouble. An employer seeing signs of these characteristics will usually want to explore the tendencies at an in-depth interview. (See 'Integrity testing' below.)

Additional information to support other selection techniques

This is the most common – and recommended – way of using personality measures. Typically, the results from a personality questionnaire will be used to support an interview, or will be added to all the other information the employer might have based on your CV, or from your performance at a presentation or from your attendance at an assessment centre.

So, for example, here you are, a well-qualified and plausible candidate for a job, you have been selected for an interview and asked to complete a personality test before you attend; how are they going to use it? The most common way is for the person who has interpreted the test to identify particular areas they want to explore with you at the interview – sometimes in person or sometimes by passing questions to the interviewer. It might be, for example, that your test profile gives a picture of you as someone who is particularly task focused and a bit of a perfectionist in your work style. While this won't rule you out (after all you have been selected for interview!) the interviewer might want to ask you about how this characteristic actually shows itself at work. Do you manage it or do you get too hung up on detail? Can you delegate or does your perfectionism mean that you try to do everything yourself? Your self-awareness comes into play again here; it will reassure the interviewer if you recognise the tendency in yourself and can show that you have developed options for mitigating any down sides.

Case study – knowing me, knowing you

Most employers who use psychometrics for middle or senior level recruitment will be particularly interested in the 'fitting in' and 'worrying signs' aspects of a potential recruit's personality. In a recent assignment we worked with an engineering employer where it was essential that a new technical specialist – Director of Research and Development - would be able to quickly fit in to an established senior team. By using a personality measure they were able to identify that the applicant with the best technical qualifications had strong preferences for independent working and for a great deal of autonomy in terms of setting the business direction. Armed with this information, the final interview panel was able to probe these areas in order to assess the difficulty this person might have in fitting in to a very cohesive team. In the end both parties agreed that the 'fit' with this particular role was not good but were able to discuss alternative jobs where this person's strengths would be better used.

Types of personality test

There is much literature on personality and personality measurement which we won't trouble you with here. (Wikipedia is a good starting place if you want to know more.) It is useful, however, to know about the main characteristics of the tests you are likely to come across.

HONESTY *IS* THE BEST POLICY

Can you 'fake' a personality test so that you appear to have characteristics that are not like you? The answer is; yes you can; but it is difficult, you will usually be caught out and ultimately it is pointless! The personality questionnaires most frequently used as part of selection procedures all have sophisticated measures of 'response bias' built in to them – psychologists' speak for 'lying through your teeth'!

In a selection situation it is understandable that people want to present themselves in the best possible light, and tests will take account of this, but they are also clever at assessing whether this is being taken to an extreme, whether there are inconsistencies in the way you respond to questions when they are put in several different ways, and whether you are trying to please the tester rather than tell the truth. In the old days, these used to be called 'lie scales' and were based on your responses to statements such as:

- I am always on time for meetings
- I have never stolen anything
- I sometimes tell lies

(We've always thought that this last item was a little paradoxical!)

These days, measures of response bias are a lot more subtle and you will tie yourself in knots trying to unravel them if you are aiming to re-spond in anything other than an honest way. So – BE YOURSELF.

Trait tests and type tests

Most of the tests you encounter in selection situations are, in the psychometric jargon, trait tests. This means that they are aiming to assess where you sit on a number of scales that are deemed relevant to your work performance; in other words where you sit in relation to relevant personality characteristics, habits or preferences.

Another category of measures are called 'type' tests; while similar in format, these tests try to assign you to a particular 'type'; in other words to group you with other people who have similar characteristics, values or preferences.

TRAIT vs TYPE

You *have* a trait (among many others) but you *fit* a type.

The most commonly used *type* test is the MBTI (Myers Briggs Type Indicator). It assigns you to one of 16 'boxes' based on your scores relating to four basic preferences. We do not recommend *type* tests for selection purposes; they are best reserved for training, development and for building self-awareness.

For the rest of this chapter we will focus on trait tests. Trait tests contain items (questions) that are relevant to work situations. Broadly, these usually cluster into questions about your:

- Thinking style
- Preferences for interacting with people
- Style in terms of delivering tasks
- Emotions

Examples of traits (characteristics) or dimensions that are included in tests are:

- Operational versus strategic
- Collaborative versus independent
- Structured versus flexible
- Obedient versus challenging

- Conceptual versus practical
- Ambitious versus contented
- Controlling versus democratic

By asking you to answer a number of questions – usually several questions per trait – the testers are trying to see what your personality profile looks like. That is, the pattern that you show in terms of all the traits. So, using the example traits listed above, a profile might look something like this:

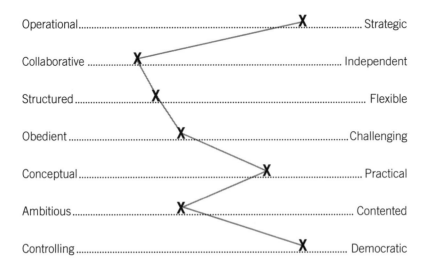

Operational	X	Strategic
Collaborative	X	Independent
Structured	X	Flexible
Obedient	X	Challenging
Conceptual	X	Practical
Ambitious	X	Contented
Controlling	X	Democratic

Test designers try to make sure that the scales are relatively independent of each other. By this we mean that you can be high, low, or average on any of the scales *regardless* of the other scales. So, the fact that you might score high on *strategic* should not influence whether you score high or low on *obedient*. (In practice, however, personality test scales often do have some small correlation with each other.)

Most of the best tests are built on the foundation of something called 'Big five' personality theory. You have already met the big five – they are the basis for the short self-completion test on page 10. Briefly, these are the five most consistent and well-researched fundamental personality characteristics that underpin a lot of our behaviour:

Openness – this refers to how open you are to new experiences, new ideas and change as well as to your intellectual curiosity.

Conscientiousness – this refers to your tendency to be organised, structured, detail conscious and reliable in meeting commitments.

Extraversion – this refers to your sociability, gregariousness, need for attention, tendency to be talkative and enthusiastic.

Agreeableness – this refers to how empathetic, understanding and keen to please you are, as opposed to tough minded and dominant.

Emotional stability – this refers to how confident, stable and emotionally cool you are as opposed to anxious and more prone to mood swings.

As ever, there are dangers in making value judgements about which ends of these scales are 'good' or 'bad'. Neuroticism in particular comes with a lot of value 'baggage', so much so that the scale is often called something else, such as confidence. When you ask people to 'fake good' in completing these tests they usually try to raise their extraversion and lower their neuroticism score but, for the reasons we have already seen, there are dangers in this. If, for example, you are somewhat stress prone, why would you seek to 'fool' an employer into giving you a job where you might continually be under pressure! So, if you try to 'fake' a low score on such anxiety or confidence scales you might not be doing yourself a favour.

Another reason for not trying to 'massage' your personality profile is that skilled interpreters of any psychometric test will not be looking at any one scale in isolation; they will be looking at combinations of factors. For example, someone who is low on conscientiousness and high on agreeableness might still be relied on to deliver because they will not want to let people down.

INTERPRETING PROFILES

The various preferences or habits we have do not operate in isolation to influence our behaviour; our traits interact with each other. For example, in terms of the Big 5 characteristics described opposite, someone who has a strong preference to be highly conscientious and rule follow-ing, who is highly agreeable and eager to please and who is also quite anxious, may make life difficult for themselves by taking on too much, by trying to deliver it somewhat perfectionistically and by becoming stressed when they can't meet all their obligations. At the same time the intro-verted but highly conscientious person need not necessarily become isolated if they recognise communication as an important part of their job description. As with all interpretations, the profile can show you the building blocks of someone's personality but only by speaking with them can you flesh this out to understand the real impact on their behaviour.

The kinds of personality measures you are most likely to encounter in selection situations will drill down from these scales into more specifically work-related characteristics. For example, agreeableness might be broken down into scales relating to autocratic versus democratic management styles, or how willing you are to take unpopular decisions.

For more details, or indeed to try out a short Big five test, visit the 'Big five personality test' website (www.outofservice.com/bigfive/) or the Signal Patterns website (www.signalpatterns.com), where you can find out how you score in terms of these characteristics. No harm in continuing to develop that self-awareness!

Reputable trait tests include:

- Occupational Personality Questionnaire (OPQ)
- Saville Consulting Wave
- Hogan Personality Inventory (HPI)
- Hogan Development Survey (HDS)
- NEO PI-R
- California Psychological Inventory (CPI)

Enter these names into your favourite search engine for more information. While there are lots of other tests, of varying quality and validity, these are the ones you are most likely to encounter.

Integrity testing

One category of personality tests focuses specifically on aspects of our personality that relate to honesty and integrity. These typically follow the standard test format but concentrate on questions about our attitudes to honesty, following rules and procedures, and about our emotions and proneness to stress.

The response bias scales in these tests are usually particularly sensitive, so again the best advice is to complete them as openly and as straightforwardly as you can.

Other measures on the market aim to explore some more extreme personality traits that research has shown to be related to career derailment or other performance problems at work. Sometimes referred to as 'dark side' characteristics, they are aspects of our 'style' or habits that we find hard to control when we are under pressure. Examples would include extreme stubbornness, perfectionism, risk taking or dominance. The HDS (mentioned above) is one example of such a measure.

Case study – managing the boss

We have already mentioned that employers are on the look out for 'worrying signs' in their recruitment processes and 'dark side' characteristics certainly provide these. Interestingly, however, many senior business leaders possess one or more dark side characteristics; for example extreme ambition or self confidence taken to the point that they find it hard to accept advice. In our experience the extent to which these characteristics represent assets or risks is often based on the resilience and indeed courage of the people working around them: again emphasising the importance of 'fit' when selecting people for senior teams. Another factor which can mitigate the risk of these characteristics is the degree of self awareness that the person shows: can they recognise those situations where their dark side characteristics might come into play and do something about it? We recently worked with a client where both of these safeguards were available and where the person in question was able to perform well.

Norming

Most of the best tests will have been tried out on a range of different people, in different jobs; this process is called 'norming'. In practice it means that an employer will not be comparing your scores with the scores of the general population, but with the scores of people in relevant comparison groups such as sales professionals, senior managers or graduates. This means that your profile or your position on a particular scale is based on how it compares with the relevant reference group and not with the general population. So, if you score 'low' on a scale relating to how ambitious you are, and the reference (or norm) group is senior managers, then this would probably mean that you are still averagely ambitious in relation to the general population but not in terms of comparison with a group of people who collectively score high in terms of ambition.

When you fill out the test or questionnaire you probably won't know which norm group is being used to provide the base line for your scores. Once again, the best advice is to be yourself rather than to answer questions in the way you think may be desirable.

Response formats

Personality tests are not usually timed (typically they take about 40 minutes). So familiarity with different response formats is much less of an issue than it is for tests of ability. However, there is no harm in being aware of the most common methods of responding.

The agree/disagree format

By far the most common response format is one where you are given a statement and then asked to indicate, using the scale provided, how much you agree or disagree with the statement. For example:

I enjoy making new friends

☐ Strongly agree
☐ Agree
☐ Don't know
☐ Disagree
☐ Strongly disagree

Most tests will encourage you to follow your gut reaction when answering the questions but it's worth pausing to think how true the statement is of you 'on average'.

Like you/not like you format

Another response format is one that 'forces' you to make choices about which ones of a series of statements are most or least like you. For example:

*For each of the statements below please indicate which **one** is most like you and which **one** is least like you. Only tick one statement in each column.*

I am the kind of person who prefers to:

	Most like me	Least like me
Work at a steady pace	☐	☐
Have a wide circle of friends	☐	☐
Have a lot of interests	☐	☐
Help people with their problems	☐	☐

This 'forced choice' format is designed to assess the relative strength of your preferences in relation to each other.

True/false format

One last format you might come across provides you – as usual – with a long list of statements, but this time you are asked to answer 'true' or 'false' to each item depending on which is most like you or which best represents your belief. For example:

	True	False
Most people are honest	☐	☐
I often feel sad	☐	☐
It is better to live life day by day	☐	☐
You should always tell people the truth	☐	☐

IN A NUTSHELL

This chapter has shown you some of the most commonly used personality and preference measures, how they are typically used and the response formats you can expect to encounter. To summarise our top tips for this chapter:

■ Be yourself.
■ Don't second-guess the test or the person who is interpreting the test; trying to give them what they want by massaging your answers will rarely pay off.
■ Think about your behaviour or your attitude 'on average' but otherwise don't worry about consistency. If you answer straightforwardly this will take care of itself.

7 PEFORMING AT YOUR BEST

This chapter is about what you can do to perform at the very best of your ability when taking a psychometric test. You will understand:

- How to develop a positive mindset

- How to get the environment right before taking a test – including having the right equipment

- Important test taking strategies such as the 'one-minute rule' and guessing wisely

- Your personal test taking style and how it could impact on your performance

Successful test taking

A key theme in this chapter is that it takes a long time to get significantly better at using numbers, understanding words or reasoning with abstract concepts. However, there are lots of reasons why people get lower test scores than they deserve.

In this chapter we explain, step by step, what you can do to avoid these pitfalls when taking psychometric tests so that your test score is your best score. Let's start with preparation and then move on to test taking.

Preparation

Becoming familiar with the various test formats

Becoming familiar with the 'look and feel' of psychometric tests, especially ability tests, is crucial. The vast majority of tests that you encounter will be in multiple-choice response format, having between four and eight possible answers to choose from. For online tests, you will be asked to check the appropriate box; for paper and pencil tests you will usually be asked to tick or shade a box on a separate answer sheet. It's always worth checking that you are putting your response in the right box. In the heat of the moment it is surprisingly easy to make a mistake, especially if you decide to skip a question, so keep checking.

It's always worth checking that you are putting your response in the right box.

Note that as well as possible answers, the options sometimes contain a 'Can't say' response (see Practice Questions). You should choose this option when the question cannot be answered from the information given; remember – it is a test of your logic and it is not meant to be an 'I don't know' option!

In Chapter 8, we have listed websites that you can use to access practice tests from most of the major test publishers. Make use of these websites, as well as those given in Chapters 4–6, to familiarise yourself with the different question and response formats.

Practising core skills

Completing psychometric ability tests involves using skills that can be practised and improved. For example:

- Numerical tests – calculating percentages
- Verbal tests – understanding word meanings
- Abstract tests – identifying different types of rules (e.g. similarities and progressions)

Case study – Martin and percentages

Martin is due to sit a numerical reasoning test in two weeks. He knows that he will have to calculate percentages to answer some of the questions. Although he knows how percentages work, it is not a skill that he often uses. Martin wants to ensure that he is as quick and error-free as possible. He identifies and regularly practises different types of percentage calculations in the run-up to taking the test (the answers are at the end of this chapter):

1. Ordinary percentages – for example, finding 35% of 5,000.
2. Increase percentages – for example, finding the previous cost of a car when it is now £15,640, which is a 15% increase on the previous cost.
3. Missing percentages – for example, if 12 of the items on sale cost less than £100 and there are 40 items in total, working out what percentage of items cost less than £100.
4. Missing whole – for example, if 20% of sales are in France and there were 50,000 sales in France, working out the total number of sales.

For a few days or weeks – while the practice is still fresh in his mind – Martin can solve these percentage problems more quickly, accurately and confidently than he normally would. Also, because he has been practising using his calculator, he knows exactly which buttons to use.

The kinds of computation required in ability tests are relatively straightforward, and most people can answer these test questions if given enough time.

However, the speed at which you complete them is important because this will affect the number of items you finish (hopefully all correctly) and so finally your score. As Martin in the case study above found, practice increases speed and accuracy.

Positive mindset

Psychological research shows that emotion has an important influence on our performance. When we are very anxious or filled with self-doubt, distracting thoughts are triggered, which take our attention away from what we are doing. These are known as performance-inhibiting thoughts, or PITs.

Compare the impact of PITs to running an unwanted application on a computer. An unwanted application takes up valuable resources such as memory and processing time which then can't be used by the computer for other, more important, tasks. PITs have the same effect on test takers.

AVOID PERFORMANCE – INHIBITING THOUGHTS, OR PITS

- Notice how much quicker and more accurate you are as you become more practised.
- Remember that some questions are designed to be very difficult – you should not expect to answer every one.
- Remember that tests are designed to have very tight timings – you may not have time to fully consider all of the questions.
- Remind yourself why you are well suited to the job you are applying for – ideally hold two or three specific reasons in your mind.
- When we are in an optimistic mindset we are more likely to perform at our best.

Communicating disabilities

If you have a disability it is important to let employers know about this before you take a psychometric test – or any type of recruitment activity. This allows employers to consider making what are known as 'reasonable adjustments', which they are legally obliged to do for certain types of disability. For more information about reasonable adjustments, see Chapter 8.

Test taking strategies

The environment

Once it is time to take the test there is some information you will be given upfront: you will be told how long the test lasts and you will be given some practice questions to complete. You might also be told how many questions there are in the test itself.

Before the test begins, it is important to check your environment. If you are completing a paper and pencil test make sure you:

- Can hear what the test administrator is saying.
- Have plenty of room – remember that you will have a question book, an answer book, rough paper, two pencils and possibly a calculator.
- Have the equipment listed above – this is usually provided by the administrator but we strongly advise you to bring your own calculator that you are fully familiar with.
- Know how to properly mark your answers in the answer sheet.
- Are comfortable and do not need a toilet break or a drink, etc.

If you are working online, make sure to check:

- That you will not be disturbed.
- That your laptop (if you are using one) is plugged into the mains.
- That your mouse or cursor control is working well.
- That you have paper and a pen or pencil available for making notes.
- That you have a calculator you are familiar with if you are completing a numerical reasoning test.
- That you are comfortable and do not need a toilet break or a drink, etc.

Timings

When you are told how long the test takes to complete note down what time you will finish. This allows you to easily check how long you have left at any point in time. Set a few simple 'check-in' points during the test. For example, if the test has 40 questions, check how you are progressing when you get to questions 10, 20 and 30. If you are halfway through the allotted time at question 15, then you know you'll need to speed-up.

The one-minute rule

If you are stuck on one question and you are losing time, remember not to panic. Instead, move on to the next question – it might suit you better. Most test scores are based on how many correct answers you have given. Read the case study below and compare John and Lisa's approach.

Case study – Effective time management while test taking

John is methodical and accurate whereas Lisa moves on when she gets stuck and guesses when she is about to run out of time. They both take a 10-question test with an eight-minute time limit.

Here is John's approach:

Question number	1	2	3	4	5	6	7	8	9	10
Time spent (in minutes and seconds)	0.31	0.25	2.26	0.49	2.55	0.52	0.02	0.00	0.00	0.00
Correct?	Yes	Yes	Yes	No	No	Yes	No	No	No	No

Total score: 4 out of 10

As expected, John worked methodically through each question. But he spent more than half of the available time answering just two questions – questions 3 and 5. He did not finish question 7 and ran out of time before he could look at the last three questions.

Here is Lisa's approach:

Question number	1	2	3	4	5	6	7	8	9	10
Time spent	0.29	0.33	0.44	0.55	0.51	0.47	0.51	1.15	0.42	0.53
Correct?	Yes	No	No	Yes	No	Yes	Yes	Yes	No	Yes

Total score: 6 out of 10

As she worked through the test Lisa realised that question 3 was very difficult and moved on to the next question. She did the same for question 5. Although she didn't answer these difficult questions correctly, she did leave herself much more time than John did to answer questions 7, 8 and 10, which were all relatively easy. She also realised that question 9 was very difficult and tried to correctly guess the answer. Overall, she was much more flexible than John in completing the test and scored two points more than him.

Lisa followed one of our test taking tips – the one-minute rule. If you are nowhere near answering a question after one minute then move on to the next. Remember, this doesn't mean that you should abandon a question that you are about to finish! The one-minute rule is about recognising when you are stuck and moving on in good time.

Guessing wisely

There are two reasons why you might need to guess the answer to a question on a psychometric ability test:

■ You can't work out the correct answer
■ You do not have enough time left to work out the answer fully.

When you do need to guess, remember that it is best not to guess randomly. Let's look at another case study.

Case study – Smart guessing in psychometric tests (1)

Kieran is taking a numerical reasoning test. One of the questions has five possible answers and only one is correct.

Credit-Flex is a loans company specialising in debt consolidation. It allows customers to pool all of their debts so that only one monthly interest payment is needed. Credit-Flex customers have loans with an average value of £5,150. Every month, customers are charged 9.25% interest on the value of their loan. Based on the average loan value, how much money in interest payments will Credit-Flex receive this month for every 1,000 customers?

A	B	C	D	E
£51,125	£476,375	£610,070	£489,875	£501,700

If Kieran makes a random guess, he has just a one in five chance of being right. By taking just a few seconds longer, Kieran can estimate the answer without performing the whole calculation. By quickly reading the question he realises that he can estimate the answer by finding 10% of £5,000, which is £500, and multiplying this by 1,000. In a few seconds he has worked out that the answer is close to £500,000. This immediately excludes options A and C which are too far away from this estimate to be correct. Without taking the time to find the precise answer he has narrowed it down to three options. In doing so, he has increased his chances of guessing correctly from one question in every five, to one question in every three.

You can use the same rules for abstract reasoning tests. Look at the next case study about a 'category'-based question (see Chapter 4 for more details about these).

Case study – Smart guessing in psychometric tests (2)

Raj is taking an abstract reasoning test as shown below.

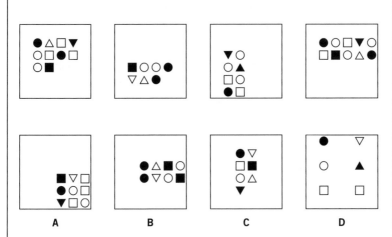

A	B	C	D

In this question there are two 'rules' in operation. The first, and most obvious, is that all of the shapes are closely grouped together. The second, less obvious rule is that there are two white shapes between every black shape, as you move from left to right and then down. From the four possible answers two are correct and two are incorrect. Raj has reached this question in the test, but he has less than 20 seconds before the time runs out, so he has to guess. One random guess gives Raj a 50% chance of choosing one of the correct options. But by spotting and using the first rule in this question – that the shapes are grouped closely together – Raj can guess smartly. He can see that option D is different from all of the other patterns because the shapes are spaced out. If he discounts this option, it gives him a 66% chance of getting one right answer.

Remember – when you need to guess don't act randomly! There are often one or two options that are obviously incorrect with just a cursory reading of the question.

Know your test taking style

What is your test taking style? And will it help you to pass a psychometric test, or might it reduce your chances? Whether you have taken psychometric tests before or if your only experience is taking school or university exams, use the questionnaire overleaf to better understand your test taking style. Simply read each statement and tick the box that best describes your approach. Complete the four sections and read our analysis and recommendations to help improve your test taking.

ACTIVITY 3

Test taking style questionnaire 1

	Strongly disagree	Disagree	Neither agree nor disagree	Agree	Strongly agree
A1	I feel that if I start answering a question I have to get it right				
A2	I am the sort of person who double checks my answers				
A3	I hate answering a question if I'm not sure what the correct answer is				
A4	Most people take less care over their work than I do				

If you **mostly agreed or strongly agreed** with the statements then you are likely to have a perfectionist test taking style that prioritises accuracy over speed. You should bear the following points in mind:

- Your natural tendency will be to preserve and get each question correct – so if you get stuck, remember to move on!
- Remember that some questions are designed to be very difficult – it is not unusual or a 'failure' if you don't know every answer.

If you **mostly disagreed or strongly disagreed** with the statements then you are likely to have an expedient test taking style that prioritises speed over accuracy. Consider the following points:

- Take care while considering which of the multiple-choice answers you select. The option that looks correct at the first glance can be incorrect.
- Make sure you know how to answer the test properly. For example, some tests require that you clearly mark a box next to your chosen multiple-choice option by completely blacking-out the appropriate box. If you are too hasty you may not indicate your choice clearly enough.

If your answers to the statements were mixed then you probably have a test taking style which balances a concern for accuracy with a willingness to work quickly.

Test taking style questionnaire 2

	Strongly disagree	Disagree	Neither agree nor disagree	Agree	Strongly agree
B1 The thought of completing a timed test makes me feel sick with nerves					
B2 I often feel anxious before important events					
B3 Sometimes I lose sleep because I feel worried					
B4 I often expect things to go wrong					

If you **mostly agreed or strongly agreed** with the statements above you are likely to have an anxious test taking style. Consider the following points:

- Excessive nervousness is distracting and can prevent you from doing your best.
- Regular practice will help you feel better prepared and calmer.
- You are not supposed to get all of the questions right – don't panic if you can't answer one, just move on!

If you **mostly disagreed or strongly disagreed** with the statements then you are likely to have a calm test taking style. Remember that:

- You will get benefit from practising extensively before taking a psychometric test. Without sufficient impetus, you may underplay the need to practise.
- If you can combine your ability to stay calm and focused with an appropriate sense of urgency in completing psychometric tests, you will be well placed to perform to the best of your ability.

If your answers to the statements were mixed then you probably have a 'keyed-up' test taking style, where you will experience a degree of nervousness and adrenaline without being overly distracted by these feelings.

Test taking style questionnaire 3

	Strongly disagree	Disagree	Neither agree nor disagree	Agree	Strongly agree
C1 When I start a test, I rarely work out how long I have to answer each question					
C2 I find it hard to keep an eye on the time as I work through a test					
C3 I often get so engrossed in the test questions that I lose all track of time					
C4 I have been surprised that I ran out of time when completing a test					

If you **mostly agreed or strongly agreed** with the statements then you are likely to have an unsystematic test taking style. Consider the following points:

■ When you are told how long the psychometric test takes to complete, note down what time you will finish. For example, if the test starts at 10.15 in the morning and takes 30 minutes to complete, write down 10.45. This allows you to easily check how long you have left at any point in time.

■ Try setting a few simple 'check-in' points during the test. For example, if the test has 30 questions, check how you are progressing when you get to questions 10 and 20. If you are halfway through the allotted time at question 10, then you know you'll need to speed up.

If you **mostly disagreed or strongly disagreed** with the statements then you are likely to have a structured test taking style. Remember the following points:

■ In your planning allow one minute at the end to guess any uncompleted questions.

■ Use your systematic approach to your advantage – if you can't answer a question, but have narrowed down the right answer to two or three of the multiple-choice options, make a quick note of these. If you finish the other questions this will allow you to focus on fewer options, or, if you run out of time and need to guess, you will have a better chance of guessing correctly.

If your answers to the statements varied, you probably have a test taking style that balances a degree of structure with some impulsivity. If this is the case, take care to check timings and progress as you complete the test, but don't allow yourself to become distracted from the test questions.

ACTIVITY 6

Test taking style questionnaire 4

	Strongly disagree	Disagree	Neither agree nor disagree	Agree	Strongly agree
D1	I like to answer test questions in the order that they are given				
D2	I expect sufficient time to complete all of the questions in a test				
D3	When completing a test I will try to complete the question I have started before moving on				
D4	I expect that I should be able to answer any question in a test correctly				

If you **mostly agreed or strongly agreed** with the statements then you have a 'traditional' test taking style. You should bear the following points in mind:

- Psychometric tests are rarely designed to be completed in the allotted time. This is done to prevent a 'ceiling effect', where too many people answer all of the questions correctly. As well as working quickly, you should be prepared to guess if you start running out of time.
- Answer the easiest questions first – this stops you getting stuck on one difficult question and running out of time. You should be fully prepared to skip difficult questions.
- Don't be concerned if you can't solve a particular question. Some questions are designed to be very difficult as another method of preventing a 'ceiling effect'. If you take it as a sign of failure, you are likely to become flustered and distract yourself. Instead, realise that it is normal to find some questions that are too difficult.

If you **mostly disagreed or strongly disagreed** with the statements then you are likely to have a flexible test taking style. Remember the following point:

- To get the best from your approach you should ensure that you move between questions in a disciplined way, rather than leaving too many questions unfinished.

If your answers to the statements were mixed then you are likely to respond flexibly to some aspects of psychometric tests, while slipping into a more formal, linear style of responding at other times. Think about when the formal approach is most likely to happen – perhaps when you are nervous, or feeling under pressure? Whatever the stimulus, remember to take a flexible approach when you can, as you will get the most benefit from answering as many questions as possible – in whatever order that entails.

Preference test tips

Completing preference tests, like personality questionnaires, is a much easier proposition than ability tests. The main point we like to emphasise is that personality questionnaires should be completed as openly and candidly as possible. We realise that there is always the temptation to second-guess what an employer is looking for – an outgoing person perhaps? Someone who has a strong attention to detail? Perhaps someone who is open to new ideas and situations?

THE PROBLEM WITH SECOND-GUESSING

- Poor fit – what if a job involves meeting new people day-in and day-out? If this would genuinely be uncomfortable for you, why pretend otherwise? A great deal of research shows that people are happier, more productive and stay longer in jobs that are well suited to their personality preferences.
- Inaccurate guessing – what you think an employer is looking for and what they are actually looking for could be entirely different! It would be most unfortunate to paint yourself in a different light if, in fact, your natural preferences are more suitable.

Other points that will help you in completing preference tests are:

- Work quickly – your 'gut instinct' is often the most accurate reflection of your true preferences. When we over-analyse our own preferences we often end up losing rather than gaining accuracy.
- Think with your 'shoes off' – we often find that the more experienced our clients are, the harder they find it to separate their 'true' preferences from the habits they have built up over many years in the workplace. To help, think about what you want to do when you get home and take your shoes off. In other words, how do you like to behave when there are no external pressures driving you – the 'shoulds' and the 'musts'. Do you seek others' company or prefer to spend some time alone? Do you make plans for the

future or tend to keep your options open? Answering in this way ensures that you reflect your natural rather than your learned style of behaving.

Answers

1. Ordinary percentages – finding 35% of 5,000. To answer this question, first find 1% of 5,000 (5,000 divided by 100, which equals 50). Then multiply 50 by 35, which equals 1,750.
2. Increase percentages – finding the previous cost of a car when it is now £15,640 which is a 15% increase on the previous cost. To answer this question we start by knowing that £15,640 is a 15% increase on an unknown figure. Another way of saying this is that £15,640 is 115% of an unknown figure. We divide £15,640 by 115, which equals £136. We then multiply £136 by 100, which gives us £13,600.
3. Missing percentages – if 12 of the items on sale cost less than £100 and there are 40 items in total, work out what percentage of items cost less than £100. There are 40 items in total so start by finding how many percentage points are represented by our smallest unit, which is one item (100 divided by 40, which equals 2.5). So if one item is 2.5% and there are 12 items costing less than £100, we then multiply 2.5 by 12 which equals 30%. So 30% of items cost less than £100.
4. Missing whole – if 20% of sales are in France and there were 50,000 sales in France, work out the total number of sales. We start by finding 1% of our missing total (50,000 divided by 20). This gives us 2,500. We then find the total by multiplying by 100, which gives 250,000 sales.

IN A NUTSHELL

There are lots of reasons why candidates get a lower score than they should on psychometric ability tests. All of these pitfalls can be avoided.

- Practise core skills such as calculating percentages and word meanings.
- Avoid performance-inhibiting thoughts through realistic test expectations and reminding yourself why you are well suited to the job.
- Set 'check points' so you can keep an eye on your progress during a test.
- Use the 'one-minute rule' – do not get stuck on difficult questions.
- Never guess randomly.
- Answer preference tests as honestly as you can – with your 'shoes off'.

8 TROUBLESHOOTING

In this chapter we focus on frequently asked questions as well as dispelling common myths and misconceptions about psychometric testing. You will understand:

■ How to access free online practice tests

■ How likely you are to receive feedback on your tests

■ What to do if you have a disability

■ The truth behind many of the most common psychometric test myths

Frequently asked questions

Where can I practise psychometric tests online?

This is by far the most popular question that candidates ask us. Getting as much practice as you can is essential and online practice tests are a great way to do this. However, be aware that the internet is awash with poor-quality sites offering almost worthless examples that will waste your time and, quite possibly, fill your inbox with spam should you register your details.

So how can you navigate your way to the most useful, safe and free practice tests? By far the best option is to start with the websites of:

- Psychometric test publishers
- University career services

Overleaf we have listed some of the most helpful websites in both of these categories. But first here is some advice for finding good quality websites.

FINDING ONLINE PRACTICE TESTS

University career services websites – which anyone can access – often have extensive and up-to-date links to all of the major test publishers that offer practice tests. Here's how to find them:

1. Go to the Google homepage – www.google.com
2. Select the 'advanced search' option
3. In the first search box (which is labelled 'find all of these words') type what you want to find. For example: 'Practice numerical reasoning' or 'Practice psychometric tests'
4. Before you start the search, go to the search box labelled 'Search within a site or domain'. In this box type '.ac.uk'. This will limit your search to universities in the UK.
5. Start the search!

Test provider websites

Kenexa online practice tests (www.psl.com/practice) – this website provides practice numerical, verbal and abstract reasoning test questions.

SHL Practice tests (www.shldirect.com/practice_tests.html) – this website includes information about tests, tips on coping with the tests, and practice verbal, numerical and abstract reasoning questions. It also includes practice personality and motivation questionnaires with free feedback.

PreVisor Talent Measurement (www.previsor.co.uk/products/certifications) – includes a wide range of sample tests on abstract, verbal and numerical reasoning.

Morrisby (www.morrisby.com – click on 'Try taking a test') – this website provides practice tests, plus guidance on test taking.

University career services

Brunel University, Placement and Careers Centre, Psychometric tests (www.brunel.ac.uk/pcc/students/psychometrictest.shtml – click on 'Try some practice tests') – this website links to a wide range of practice tests from test publishers and employers.

University of Kent, How to pass graduate aptitude tests (www.kent.ac.uk/careers/psychotests.htm) – you can practise on a range of tests that were developed specifically by the university.

Imperial College Business School, Psychometric tests (www3.imperial.ac.uk/business-school/currentstudents/careers/career_process/accessingopportunities/psychometric – click on 'online example tests') – this website has links to practice tests from major test publishers, as well as employers such as the Civil Service, Barclays Capital and McKinsey.

University of Liverpool, Centre for Lifelong Learning, Practice Psychometric Tests Online (www.liv.ac.uk/careers/students/cvs_applications_interviews/psychometric/links.htm) – this website has links to a variety of ability and personality-based psychometric tests.

Other resources

IQtext.dk (http://iqtest.dk/main.swf) – this website has a good-quality, free abstract reasoning test that produces an IQ score.

AssessmentDay (www.assessmentday.co.uk) – this website has free practice questions for numerical, verbal and abstract reasoning.

How long do psychometric tests take to complete?

Ability tests such as verbal, numerical and abstract reasoning always have strict time limits. These vary between tests although most have a time limit of between 20 and 50 minutes. Tests of preference are almost always untimed and will take around 30 minutes to complete if you work at a reasonable pace.

Will I get feedback or see my results?

This depends on two factors – the type of test you are taking and the recruitment environment that you are in. Table 8.1 describes the key differences:

Table 8.1

	Recruitment environment which has one or more of the following:	Recruitment environment which has one or more of the following:
	■ High volume of candidates	■ Few candidates
	■ Psychometrics as an early screening method	■ Psychometrics as part of a wider assessment event
	■ Only external candidates	■ Many internal candidates
	■ Junior management positions or lower	■ Senior and executive positions
Ability tests	No feedback or results beyond a 'pass' or 'fail' decision	A description of the comparison group used (e.g. UK-based managers and professionals) and a quantitative or qualitative result (e.g. '55th percentile' or 'typical of most other managers and professionals')

	Recruitment environment which has one or more of the following:	Recruitment environment which has one or more of the following:
	■ High volume of candidates	■ Few candidates
	■ Psychometrics as an early screening method	■ Psychometrics as part of a wider assessment event
	■ Only external candidates	■ Many internal candidates
	■ Junior management positions or lower	■ Senior and executive positions
Preference tests	Often no explicit reference to the results. At best a computer-generated report or profile	A detailed feedback discussion which explains what the questionnaire measures and how your preferences are likely to affect the job in question

Who scores psychometric tests?

Many modern psychometric tests are designed to be computer scored. It is a sobering thought that when you complete an online test there is a computer server, somewhere in the world, that records your score just seconds after you have finished. Interestingly, although many of these systems could email your results back to you moments after you have finished, almost all have an in-built delay of days or even weeks. It seems to be a universal truth that if we have failed a test, we want to think that someone, somewhere, spent time considering our efforts before casting us aside!

If you complete a pencil-and-paper test someone who is specifically trained to administer and score psychometric tests will calculate your results. Test publishers are very concerned about the integrity and security of their products and, as a result, there are rigorous guidelines about who is allowed to administer and score psychometric tests.

How effective are psychometric tests for recruitment?

A great deal depends on the nature of the psychometric test and the nature of the job you are applying for. A large body of research has shown that ability-based psychometric tests are very good predictors of real-life job performance across almost all job roles and especially those with a high degree of complexity.

Preference-based psychometric tests have also been shown to predict aspects of job performance well, although they are more dependent upon skilful interpretation, for example, in order to identify the most relevant questions to use at interview. Like any other tool, psychometric tests are most effective when they are well matched to the task at hand, as the hammer to the nail.

How seriously do employers take the results of psychometric tests?

In our experience, the vast majority of employers take the results very seriously. This is especially true with online recruitment where organisations use the results to make automatic decisions about whom to invite to the next stage and whom to reject.

What if my personality profile is 'straight down the middle', with no particular high or low characteristics; will they think I am uninteresting?

Anyone with proper training interpreting such test scores will recognise that mid range scores do not mean boring! What they mean is that your habits or preferences are not so strong that you will have particular 'default' behaviours in any given situation. Instead you will have options about which way you are likely to respond. For example, if you have a mid-range score on a characteristic such as openness to experience, it suggests that there will be times when you behave in a relatively adventurous way and other times when you are more cautious. In our experience, it is less likely to mean that you are averagely open to experience across all situations.

What if I am unhappy with the way my test results or profile come out?

It is always possible that you have misinterpreted the scoring or rating instructions or that you have completed the test in a hurry or when you were distracted. On the other hand it may be that you are the kind of person who does not spend a lot of time thinking about their style and who finds the resulting profile hard to interpret. If you find yourself in a situation where you really do not recognise the person described by the test results, try to think about what might have gone wrong. It is unlikely – but not impossible – that the test scorer has made a mistake; it is more likely that something has interfered with your ability to complete the test accurately – for example, doing it in a rush. If this happens then it is worth pointing it out to the person who is using the test but it is best to avoid sounding defensive. If there really is a strong mismatch between the test results and your perception of yourself, then you can always offer to take the measure again. After all, the person using the test is just as interested in getting an accurate picture as you are.

What if I don't have internet access for online tests?

Many organisations have introduced online tests as part of the applications process, especially when there are large numbers of candidates. In almost all of these cases paper versions of the tests are not available and you will need to have access to an internet-enabled computer. Many local libraries offer free or low-cost internet access, and it is also worth checking if your friends or relatives have internet access. Whichever option you consider, remember that you will ideally need a quiet environment where you can concentrate without being disturbed.

What if I have a disability?

When using psychometric tests, employers should ask candidates to indicate whether they have a disability. This is important because employers can then make what are known as 'reasonable adjustments'. For example, a candidate with a visual impairment could be given a large-text version of the test, or a candidate with dyslexia might be given additional time to complete the test. If you do have a disability make sure that you inform the employer before you complete any psychometric tests – or indeed any other part of a selection process.

Legally, employers cannot discriminate against a candidate with a disability and knowing about a disability allows employers to liaise with a candidate to discuss what reasonable adjustments can be made.

As the head of recruitment at a government department has emphasised to us 'Our priority is recruiting the best people and our tests should not be a barrier for candidates with disabilities. We actively encourage our candidates to get in touch if they need to discuss any adjustments.'

Myths and misconceptions

"We look at the internet forums, and you see some really wild speculation about the tests that firms use. It's completely wrong and doesn't help anyone." (Graduate recruiter, UK law firm).

The results of preference tests are meaningless – people's personalities change all the time

Although we all vary our behaviour from situation to situation, it is well proven that there are consistent patterns to the way we think and act – and that is our personality. Some of us are very reliable, others less so. Some are keen to impress, whereas others are unconcerned about social standing.

By early adulthood we all have a fairly settled set of preferences which define our personality. Although these preferences can and do change over time these changes are mostly subtle. As a result, psychometric tests can measure our preferences in a meaningful and useful way.

People can cheat at ability tests by taking them several times

Test publishers are very aware of the risk of cheating and they have developed several methods to prevent it. Paper-based tests almost all have 'parallel forms'; these are multiple versions of the same test which have similar but different questions. These tests are carefully designed so they are equivalent – one version has the same degree of difficultly as the other. Therefore, you may know some of the answers to 'form A', but next time you might sit the test you may be given 'form C'.

Online ability tests employ a technique called 'item banking', which is a more flexible version of parallel forms. Let's say that a numerical ability test has 30 questions. The test publisher creates a 'bank' of 300 questions, which are carefully assessed so that each question has a known level of difficulty. When you complete that numerical test online a computer randomly draws 30 questions from the bank of 300 for you to complete. As a result, many candidates can complete the test and each one will have different questions. Importantly, each test will be of equivalent difficulty so that the scores can be meaningfully compared.

If you don't know the answer, always guess 'C'

When you complete an ability-based psychometric test, you will almost certainly have to guess some of the multiple-choice answers. Whether or not it is option 'C', many people subscribe to the view that by consistently guessing the same option, you are bound to get at least some questions correct.

To reinforce a point we made in Chapter 7, it is much better to guess wisely than to guess randomly. A wise guess can simply involve taking 10 seconds to spot that options D and E are definitely not the right answer. If there are five possible answers, then that wise guess will give you a 33% chance of being right – as opposed to just a 20% chance through random guessing (even if there is a consistency to your randomness!).

9 AND FINALLY...

Preparation makes no difference, you've either got it or you haven't

A key theme of this book is that there are lots of reasons for getting a score lower than you deserve. These include:

- Lack of familiarity with psychometric tests
- Anxiety
- Poor test taking strategy
- Lack of practice

It is important to recognise that all of these reasons can be influenced. By taking action to prepare effectively you will be able to perform to the best of your abilities.

Psychometric tests are being used more often than ever by employers to recruit and promote staff. As a result, people who can pass these tests are in stronger positions to secure the jobs they want.

By reading this book and completing the practice questions you have already taken a significant step to performing at your very best when completing psychometric tests. You now know:

■ How psychometric tests work – there is no 'black magic' and nothing to be afraid of!
■ How to prepare yourself and your environment
■ What the test questions look like and how to complete them
■ About your own test taking style
■ Where to access online practice tests

When we started writing this book we knew that many candidates under preformed on psychometric tests, for a variety of reasons. With that in mind our aim was to give clear, easy to use advice, which will help candidates to show employers what they are really capable of.

An interesting side-effect is this: when candidates complete psychometric tests to the very best of their ability, it means that employers make better decisions because the scores they have are entirely accurate. Now that's a win–win.

The knowledge and confidence you will have gained from using this book means that when you complete psychometric tests in the future your concentration will be focused on answering the questions and you will not be distracted by uncertainty or over anxiety.

These skills of test taking will be useful to you throughout your career whether you are joining a new employer, competing for internal positions, or engaging in a talent management process.

We leave you with the reminder that it is often the most well prepared who succeed in passing psychometric tests. With this in mind we wish you all the best!

Ceri Roderick and James Meachin
www.pearnkandola.com

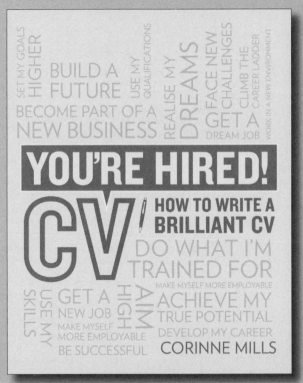